READ THE ROOM

READ THE ROOM

The Holistic Guide to Build and Sustain Meaningful Relationships for Life

CAVANAUGH JAMES

BenBella Books, Inc.
Dallas, TX

BENBELLA

BenBella Books, Inc.
10440 N. Central Expressway
Suite 800
Dallas, TX 75231
benbellabooks.com
Send feedback to feedback@benbellabooks.com

BenBella is a federally registered trademark.

Printed in the United States of America
10 9 8 7 6 5 4 3 2 1

Library of Congress Control Number: 2023042805
ISBN (hardcover) 9781637744529
ISBN (electronic) 9781637744536

Editing by Rachel Phares
Copyediting by Elizabeth Degenhard
Proofreading by Sarah Vostok and Jenny Bridges
Illustrations by Joseph Noble
Text design and composition by Jordan Kolouch
Cover design by Brigid Pearson
Printed by Lake Book Manufacturing

For each person who has planted a seed in my life,
giving beyond themselves.
For each friend who cultivated character
with selflessness and empathy.
This book is your garden, grown up and out,
a canopy over each page.

Contents

Foreword

I'VE NEVER WRITTEN THE FOREWORD to a book before. But I've also never had a friend quite like Cavanaugh James. The benefits of a friend like Cavanaugh are immeasurable, and I know that you, too, will find his friendship through this book valuable.

Reading this book, I found myself listening to his voice and nodding my head. This is it. This is who he is. This is what he adds to my life and the lives of so many others. Since I've mentioned that you will be his friend, maybe I should tell you how he became mine.

One thing that has been annoyingly consistent in our almost fifteen-year friendship is that Cavanaugh and I remember the meat and potatoes of a story the same. But every now and again, like all friends do, we get hung up on inconsequential details and our "healthy" younger sibling competitive spirit makes things like remembering the name of the restaurant we went to in that small town in Colorado, or what movie we watched on the Fourth of July 2017, or who said what to piss the other off, all the more taxing when trying to retell the story of how we became friends. To put it simply, it was fate . . . which really means our mothers pushed us to hang out.

There are two things to clarify about the information in the previous paragraph: first, my version of said events is accurate. Second, yes, our mothers told us we should hang out. That tells you a lot about where we both were during that point in our lives and our confidence (or wariness) in making new friends.

My two brothers and I had just experienced a wonderful, albeit disorienting, meteoric rise in our music career and our family had also just moved into a new home in a quiet neighborhood in Dallas, Texas, to seek some peace and normalcy. Our parents were rightfully concerned that their three newly famous teen sons, and their almost six-and-a-half-year-old firecracker, Franklin, would lose touch with their values if the family lived in Los Angeles or New York. This move made sense for many reasons, and we also had roots in Dallas. Our parents met there at Bible college in the eighties. They went on to work at that same Bible college in various capacities after being students, and eventually, after a somewhat short-lived youth pastoring gig in New Jersey, the family settled back in Texas where I was born.

Flash forward to 2008. At this point I was fourteen and trying to balance the very isolating feeling of experiencing adrenaline-infused highs after a concert or a promo run with the quiet normalcy of the new neighborhood we pulled our not-so-subtle black and white tour bus into each day. It's safe to say the neighbors would have been well within their rights to be agitated by this sudden disruption, but what we found was the exact opposite.

It sounds funny even now, all these years later, to think that one of my soon-to-be best friends in the world would just happen to be my literal next-door neighbor. I'm a strong believer in being in the right place at right time, and destiny; however, I didn't think these things just happened, and I certainly didn't think they'd happen to me.

I was very closed off at this stage in my life. I had a core group of friends, all people I worked with, and that was all I thought I needed. I was wrong.

My version of the story is that we played basketball the first time we hung out. He says we met at my house or something, said a quick hello and then we went our separate ways. The truth is, it doesn't matter.

After getting over the initial awkward mom set-up, Cavanaugh and I started hanging out, and we haven't stopped or looked back ever since. We've traveled the world together, had deep conversations about life, family, relationships, faith, marriage, and fatherhood. We've celebrated one another, we've been angry with one another, and we've both challenged each other to pick ourselves up off the floor, dust off, and be the people we know we're called to be when life knocks us down.

Shortly after he served as a groomsman in my wedding to my brilliant better half, Priyanka (or Pri as I call her), the three of us were sitting on the back porch of my home with Pri in Los Angeles when Cavanaugh shared his idea for this book and its accompanying podcast with us. We were both over the moon that the world would finally get to hear what we have been fortunate enough to hear and personally benefit from for so long, just by doing life with Cavanaugh.

When it comes to relationships of all kinds, whether they be family, friends, business, or romantic, there is no one more thoughtful and understanding than Cavanaugh. His professional and personal experiences make him uniquely qualified to write this book, and I know that as you dive in you will see your awareness and thoughtfulness in communication with the people in your life personally and professionally improve ten-fold.

The same qualities that make Cavanaugh a reliable friend, brother and son are what make him successful when it comes to understanding people. Often we are so caught up in our own world, focused on our own challenges and disappointments, that we lose sight of what really matters. This book will provide tools that you will use daily. Or, even if you might already have them, you might not have been mentored and learned how to use them. And isn't that the important part?

So gear up for an unimaginably enjoyable ride. You'll laugh, you'll cry and you'll learn just how beneficial it is to *Read the Room*.

—Nick Jonas

Introduction

SO YOU WALK INTO A room full of people you hardly know—it might be a work gathering, a party a friend invited you to, or a meetup with new neighbors after moving—and you have no idea what to do first. It's an overwhelmingly terrifying moment we all know well, and one that may incite feelings of social anxiety just reading about it. How can you minimize your discomfort? Should you visit the buffet table? You could snag a cream puff or two to occupy your hands and mouth for a bit. It's hard to expect small talk from someone with a mouthful, after all, right? Sure, you could find a group of friendly faces and stand on the outskirts of their circle hoping to be invited in. But what happens if you're just left hovering and lingering for a minute or two too long? Oh, the excruciation. At this point, after you've gone through scenario after panic-inducing scenario, you begin looking for a corner to hover in—thinking, of course, that you could just walk back out the way you came. But will you instead choose to lean in to others (and lean out of yourself*) and read the room?

You scan the room looking for a clue to light your next step and then you accidentally lock eyes with someone. That person smiles. You smile back thankfully. That person makes a quick perusal of the room and then looks back at you, summing up your situation in a heartbeat. With a lift of their chin that lets you know they know just how you feel and want to help you break the ice, that person informally invites you to join their group.

Grateful, you smile again and cross the room. Once you're there, that person introduces themself, asks your name, and introduces you to the rest of the people in the circle. Your heart rate lowers enough for you to be present with your new acquaintances.

The person you locked eyes with casually asks you a few questions about yourself until there is a touch point with someone else in the group. They point it out and introduce you two, and the connecting point becomes common ground to build on. You ask your newest friend a question, they answer in a way that shows genuine interest, and then ask something compelling back—a conversation happens.

In a matter of seconds, you've gone from being an outsider to the group to a participant just as naturally as you would have found

---

* A note for readers: throughout this book, we'll talk about both "leaning in" and "leaning out." We'll discuss these concepts in greater detail later on, but for now, it'll be helpful for you to know how I'm using these terms throughout the book. "Leaning out" means looking outward (leaning *out* of yourself) and "leaning in" refers to an intentional, other-focused point of view (leaning *in* to the people and world around you). These are actually two sides of the same coin, and later on, you'll see that they're used somewhat interchangeably.

a friend to play with on the playground when you were six. You start to relax and settle in; so do your nerves.

When you get a chance again to catch the eye of the person who first invited you over, you smile a bit of your gratitude. They give you an "it was nothing" shrug. You give an appreciative chuckle and go back to trying to follow the hot-potato game of conversation going on around you. You start to feel like you belong and wait for your chance to join in. You soon realize you're having actual fun—all because someone chose to lean out of their social comfort long enough to see you and bring you into theirs.

Chances are, if I had been there, I would've liked to be the person who smiled and invited you over—to be your bridge to a new situation. Depending on the environment, I may have even yelled, with love, "Hey, friend, come on in—the water's fine!"

I've had to do my fair share of socially "sinking or swimming," and now, my life's passion and burn is to help others swim well with others. But who am I to be delivering a book to you on interpersonal relationships?

Well, for starters, my professional life (and success) largely centers around relationships—I have gravitated toward work that allows me to use and hone my own authentic relational skills and work that helps others improve their own. First, I consult for organizations—and individuals within those organizations—of varying sizes, helping them to create relationally healthy workplaces. You'll read stories of that consulting work as well as other clear examples of actual people (me included) as we move through this book. I also cofounded You and Me Media, a growing media company that serves podcast creators' needs, from daily tasks to big-picture strategy. And finally, I have an extensive background in the music and entertainment industry. I've now spent well over a decade intimately involved with supporting artists and performers in various lanes by first choosing to be a friend, stewarding that friendship, and then eventually being recognized as a safe place to work out often tedious and special relational dynamics. This was not something I sought out. However, I love to champion others and I don't play around with honesty—two qualities lacking a bit within the industry. For these reasons, and thanks to my deep disdain for ulterior motives and manipulation, I've been given a place from which to speak into the lives of people I greatly respect and love, many of whom happen to work in entertainment and other public-facing vocations. At the end of the day, in nearly every aspect of my personal and professional life, I am cultivating relationships. And let me tell you—I've learned a lot along the way.

None of this means I wear some plastered smile and show up in the lives of others with the iridescent oily sheen of a "yes" person. It means I show up authentically, as I am, positioned to see every person and situation holistically—as whole, nuanced, and utterly complicated. May I tell you what I've learned from my seat? That the principles that support healthy relationships are consistent and transferable, no matter your situation. We all navigate different life circumstances, different people, different power dynamics, and different experiences. But the keys to cultivating and sustaining relationships—in any area of life—are more universal than you might realize.

My desire is to help provide you with tools and strategies to be confident and comfortable in your character, motive, and execution of any relationship. I don't want you to just be a person who can spot someone needing a friend at a party; I want you to take ownership of how you steward people and to be an initiator of relational and personal health in the lives you touch. You now have my destination in mind, but where you actually end up relationally is entirely up to you.

Have you ever gone to an event, gathering, or function for one reason only to find a litany of others once you're there? You might meet a new collaborator, connect with a friend you didn't think you'd see, have a conversation that inspires your next career move, or maybe even lock eyes with someone you end up giving your heart to. But the entry points for unexpected goodness like that are often found in relational skills such as awareness of an environment, curiosity of another person, or merely just an empathetic lens with which to have a conversation.

What you'll realize over the course of this book, if you don't already, is that relationships are the doorway to everything genuinely good in life: the doorway to opportunities, to friends who are like family, to finding the right job, to getting a promotion, to finding a spouse, and so much else. They are also critical to our well-being. There is a vast amount of research, I mean hundreds of articles in the academic community, to this point. Relationships can contribute to the health or deterioration of a person's physical and mental condition. Those who have strong relational bonds, regardless of whether they're platonic, romantic, friendly, or merely communal, experience legitimate health benefits. These benefits show up when someone deeply connected to others falls sick with disease or is trying to recover from injury or an operation—healthy relationships can help bolster a stronger immune system and lead to faster physical healing. Research even shows that strong relationships can help bring about lower rates of depression and anxiety.

The trouble is, we live in an age where friendship has been reduced to checking a box on a social media app, and where intimacy is often exchanged for what's easiest. But "following" from a distance and genuinely sharing life with another, along with its speed bumps and hurdles, are vastly different ventures. I fear we've come to accidentally conflate "friend" with "follower," and think of relationships more in terms of a quantity of "likes" than a quality of character you can count on when the chips are down.

The art of reading a room—of recognizing people for who they are, helping them connect where they should, and being a friend in the process—is getting smothered in our fast-paced, "please like and follow" world today. Without our realizing it, "influencer" culture has crept into our vernacular, informing how we pose for pictures, how we position ourselves socially, even the tonality we invoke when sharing vulnerability. I don't deem this shift all horrible; rather, I see it as worthy of examination.

I've had to examine the unhealthy cultural rhythms I've picked up; in many cases, over time, I've managed to uproot their influence in my life. This has greatly improved my relationships and my ability to authentically connect with people. It's taken trial, error, and real time. It's taken me getting it wrong a lot so you can get it wrong a lot less, and I would like to use my learning experience to clear a pathway of understanding for you to do the same. Our fullest life begins the second we realize we're not the only one in it. It's all about seeing, hearing, and getting to know others, and then helping each other find their best. It's about having real conversations. It's about learning to build mutual trust. It's about working through the tough stuff so when the pressures of success or failure squeeze us, we're not alone, and we can pull together to see each other through to the other side.

It might sound a little strange, but if we were to think of having healthy relationships in similar terms to having a healthy body, this book would be chock-full of superfoods meant to make your relational world strong, healthy, active. They're meant to jump-start an exercise routine of sorts, one that will build and tone your relational muscles.

That means sometimes it will be blueberries, sometimes it will be kale, and other times it'll be a sweaty workout that leaves you a little sore, but I'll tell you now, you'll be glad to go through it because of how it will pay off. Of course, comparing relational health to healthy foods and habits means we have to acknowledge the flip side: that there are "junk foods" in our relationships and habits alike. For instance, gossiping with someone about a messy situation at work may feel fun and enjoyable in the moment, but it provides as much relational nutrition to you and your friend as a bag of Sour Patch Kids. On the other hand, exchanging that gossip for an engaged conversation with the person in question not only tastes better, it invests in the health of your relationship, too. Changing the relational tools we use on a whim and reorienting our relational taste buds is the actual workout. Care to work out together?

You'll feel great, all while creating a healthier pattern of being. If you've ever tried to change your eating habits to support a healthier lifestyle, you might know that feeling when you begin to crave and actually look forward to foods you once forced yourself to consume. Carrots with hummus, on paper, might not be your pick over a delicious bag of chips. However, upon making yourself enjoy the carrots and hummus in lieu of the chips and noting how your body responds, you pair a result with a corresponding action. I feel better when I eat carrots than when I eat chips. This helps reorient your taste buds. Now, chips will always taste good . . . crack open my cabinets and you'll find evidence to that fact. But what tastes good and what genuinely serves the body in health are often different things. So we're going to reorient our taste buds together.

I believe once you know what this health looks like in your own life and how to bring a transferable level of that health with you into relationships with others, you will see no end to the benefits of all the hard relational work.

Dreams don't happen in isolation. It takes a village—it takes a community—and you'll need to learn how to make good friends to build such a community. It's just the way the world works, though it's not really what the world teaches you about how to succeed. Our culture and society team up and convince us that success looks like advocating for ourselves beyond all others, but I've found that self-centered approach to be confusing, misleading, and a direct route to breakdown. It's also just an exhausting way to live.

However, we're culturally told to take this route. We're trained to look out for our own desires and expect results immediately. Simply look at the number of apps designed to get you what you want, exactly when and how you want it. Look at the average advertisement and the lyrics of many Top 40 songs. An overarching theme you'll encounter, a message we're constantly fed, is to focus on oneself. It might be framed as self-empowerment, a desire for love, a fear of rejection, what's "deserved," or simply a need to be authentically oneself. I love snappy messaging and catchy songs just as much as the next person, and true self-awareness is actually a crucial part of healthy relationships (more on this later). But in our lives, the kind of one-dimensional self-focus we're taught to value is a corrosive toxin that spoils anything it touches.

I'd like to clear up that confusion for you, that line of thinking that might say, "Focusing on me is the only way I'll actually get what I want in life." I certainly understand that thought and have put it to use in my own life plenty of times—in my actions at work, in my relationships, and absolutely in my conversations. However, when I do, I'm left with less of what I want—real, authentic connection—than I had before. But now, what I genuinely want is to set you up to win in a people-focused life despite being conditioned to win in a me-focused life, which, in the end, is really no fun (nor is it really winning). If you'll allow me, I'd like to walk you into some new thinking that will open you up to the world and the other people in it in some compelling ways you may never have considered before.

Think of reading this book as if we've chosen to spend an evening together at a beautiful little two-story café. As you walk up the staircase, you find me sitting in a cozy booth . . . I imagine there to be floor-to-ceiling green velvet curtains enveloping our table, with your favorite beverage and some choice snacks awaiting your arrival. Here, in this booth, we have the freedom to be comfortable, honest, and vulnerable. Maybe it looks something like this.

During our time at this cozy café, we're going to give each other the permission to be exactly who we are—and where we are—in life. I'm going to crack some jokes, we're going to have some knowing laughs and *aha* moments together, but it's going to be real. It's only from this authentic place I'm even willing to write, so I invite you to join me. I am confident this book is supposed to be in your hands, right now, for this exact moment.

During our time together we're going to look at selfishness, where it shows up in our actions and lives, and why it costs us. Then we're going to slowly exchange the unhealthy relational tools we recognize in ourselves for empathetic ways to build bridges between people, close gaps of understanding and connection, and lead others into healthier relational dynamics. Once we truly reorient how we see a room, our motivation for doing so, and what we're looking for when we do, we can read it. More than a quick guide of body language and corresponding meanings, this is a comprehensive look at healthy relational functioning and why it's so crucial to our well-being.

It's a passion for people being seen, loved into healthier rhythms, and alive in their relationships that's led me to spend this time—this book—with you. But there's absolutely a genesis to how I came to burn for people the way I do. I think it began when someone was willing to take the time to lean out of themselves and meet me in the middle of a precarious dynamic.

Let me tell you that story.

1

Lean Out

IN ELEMENTARY SCHOOL, RECESS WAS never my favorite part of the day.

I grew up in Texas, and for me, recess was always a guarantee of three things: sweating, exhaustion, and a smattering of bullying. My interests in creativity (and all its expressions) over athletics made for a less than peaceful time at school where most of the boys my age flowed in the opposite direction. I also wasn't the most physically active child, period. That is, if you don't count the speed with which I could take down two bags of Hot Fries at lunch. Athleticism should be celebrated wherever it's found, and an elementary cafeteria is a coliseum as far as I'm concerned. Regardless, it was at this stage of my life that I realized being any kind of different comes with its own costs. While I'm now happy to pay those costs, at that time it made me feel like an outsider and a bit of a freak.

And I might have stayed feeling that way, had it not been for Ms. Prego.

Ms. Prego was my fifth grade teacher, and she would come out with us during recess. As I look back, I realize that was probably supposed to be a bit of "off" time for her, as opposed to the "on" time of teaching and keeping kids focused on the right things. But Ms. Prego didn't disengage. Instead, she stayed observant and intervened when she thought it was necessary.

And thanks to Ms. Prego, what I remember most about elementary school isn't the not-so-kind comments made by a couple of other kids. What I think of first is my teacher who was, for all intents and purposes, my first investor outside of my parents. She was an incredible educator. And more than that, she was deeply aware.

She was the first teacher I had who actually saw and understood how I was being treated by others in my class. She intuitively knew why I loathed recess, realizing it was more than my aversion to heat. So when we went outside and I started to get picked on, she would call me over. Then we would stand and talk for the remainder of recess.

She told me stories about growing up in Nicaragua before and during its revolution. She told me about her family, how she missed them, and how our class had become a sort of family to her. She lived on Lake Nicaragua and would tell me stories of bull sharks who had learned to swim inland in the fresh water . . . which timed perfectly with my discovery and simultaneous fandom/fear of *Jaws* (the original and all three sequels). She would ask me about things I was interested in and allowed me to share whatever I wanted. She listened with earnest curiosity to my obsessions with theater and roller coasters. (Oh, I was a *very* cool fifth grader.) We would laugh together and for those few minutes, I genuinely had a friend.

When the bell rang and we headed back inside, the dread I had felt when we'd headed out the door was gone. The sweat still fell, but at least I felt confident and a bit lighter on my feet while laying my head on my desk trying to return my body to its "normal" temperature. By taking a few minutes to talk with me, she transformed a moment that might have gotten ugly into something affirming. She created a safe place for me.

Ms. Prego didn't have to notice me in the middle of a precarious social situation at school. I was one student of many, and I'm certain recess could have been thirty minutes of much needed peace and quiet for her. Instead, she was sensitive enough to be aware and make me feel good about my unique likes and dreams, even if they flowed against the grain of most of her other students. She didn't treat me as the problem or an exception. Rather, she made a protected place for me and, in turn, set me up for a win in life by showing me such identifiable kindness.

In a similar way, as an adult, I'm often concerned with setting myself and others up for a "win" whenever possible. Truthfully, we're constantly setting ourselves up for *something* depending on how we choose to interact with people, but the outcome is up to us. The choices we make matter.

One of the places I continually learn this is in any backstage role on tour. I've been fortunate to tour in a variety of ways with different artists, but the commonality I've seen is clear. Tours are self-sustaining mini cities on the move. Stage crews do an incredible amount of work, and there's a lot of pressure to set up and tear down in a timely manner for each show. Each member of the crew fulfills a role (or multiple roles) that serves the entire mechanism. Although there may be pockets of free time on the road, more than seeing people hang out and catch their breath, you will see a volley of teamwork, a dance of sorts. Everyone has a contribution to give and when they don't, others are left making up for that lack. Where other working environments might welcome you to kick your feet up and relax in the specificity of a role, traveling on the road requires you be sat up, at attention, and ready to move where needed. Now, will you see everyone operate from this mentality? No, no you will not. However, in other places the one who "does the most" might be an outlier among coworkers and stick out in the culture. Here, the one unwilling to step in, to see and meet a need, or to fulfill another needed role for the moment is the one who sticks out. And this can teach us a lot about how promotion and advancement in our jobs are often tied to an ability to see a whole environment, pivot according to the current needs of that environment, and be relationally focused in the process.

If we could, I'd take you backstage on a tour, and you and I could plop down on a road case in the hallway and be endlessly fascinated by the social structure. Over the years, this is where I've seen some of the clearest examples of people either setting themselves up for relational wins or relational losses. Although these moving cities carry a culture unique to themselves, the principles that advance people upward or downward in that culture are universal.

Those who are promoted are the ones willing to be a Swiss Army knife of usefulness. Regardless of what someone's role is, they earn respect in how they treat and are aware of others. It doesn't matter if you're a guitar tech, a road manager, working the merch table, or onstage every night. I have watched countless assistants, crew members, and musicians be promoted or replaced almost solely based on the ways they engaged with others. Yes, efficiency, skill level, and effectiveness all contribute, but the ways we treat people either propel us forward or hold us back.

In a working environment, or in any environment, really, we are drawn to those we respect on a relational level. We want to work with people we feel are team players and who aren't merely chasing their own trophies. We don't want to spend every day with coworkers who exist like islands unto themselves, unaware and uncaring of how they make others feel. We trust people who prioritize making others look good, those willing to make a relational effort, and the ones who do it all with kindness.

Certainly, our specific gifts make a place for us in any situation, and some seem gifted enough that exercising their talents is all they need, but I've never seen such people be very happy. Often the littlest thing can push them over the edge. It takes a lot of money, influence, and real gall to try to make up for bad relationship skills. Those who implement this strategy of self-absorption in trying to impress and position rather than connect where people are concerned only make it work for them for short and cyclical moments. And in the end? None of it fulfills what real relationships do. It won't build trust or authenticity or real connection. And that's where joyful life is.

What I've seen to be true is that kindness and being willing to do what is needed, even if it's not in your job description, go further than talent alone, and those who exercise these character traits enjoy the journey more than those who go it alone. In every interaction, we have the constant choice to extract from others or invest in them, and while the first provides a short-term gain, investing in others leads to the most incredible places. You never know how far even a small investment can go—or how big it might return.

But it takes some self-awareness to live a life of investing in others and a sense of identity that is flexible and confident enough to lean out and away from its own needs to help someone else meet theirs. The truth is, though, most of us aren't raised with those necessary skills. We grow up to some degree or another in an identity crisis, and we're often so wrapped up in figuring out who we are that we've little room to be aware of what's going on with anyone else.

Although Ms. Prego stopped to invest in me all those years ago, I had to grow and understand for myself what she knew and lived out seamlessly. People are longing to be met with kindness and awareness. It's crucial, in fact. The way she reached me by simply giving me a safe place is the way I want to meet everyone—like a glass of cool water waiting in the shade. But that didn't keep me from living many years as someone so wrapped up in myself I couldn't see anyone else in the room. The seeds people sow by way of investing in our lives often grow in us at peculiar rates. I'm grateful that seed from Ms. Prego's kindness was planted in my life, because it's grown in me a wealth of fruit I've been able to share with others. Now my hope is to deposit a portion of that investment in *your* life.

Discovering My Lean

I grew up as a fairly creative kid who wanted to be onstage and involved in every corner of the theatrical world. My family and surroundings were full of love, and I think back with a great deal of fondness to much of my upbringing. But problems and discomfort inevitably invade most environments, as I know you've probably experienced for yourself.

I'm from a rather big family and, because I came last, I grew up in an already established, well-oiled machine that succeeded in athletics and almost every sort of outdoor activity. It was no surprise that I was encouraged to follow suit and sort myself into a sport I excelled at. I was less than excited about this as I grew up, and, as a result, I seldom felt I belonged. As anyone who feels they're the odd bird in their family might find, trying to simultaneously be yourself and also emulate what you've seen modeled and championed around you can feel like wearing a suit or a dress that was actually made for an older sibling with a different body type. It's too big, yes, but also pinches in all the wrong places. It's not the best look.

I often felt as if I spoke a different language from my siblings, and I think they may have found me difficult to relate to or understand because of it. They were of course figuring themselves out, too, and we did our best to meet each other where we were. They loved me well, but not without puzzled looks from time to time—which was fair. I sent my own share of looks their way, after all. My daily task, as I saw it, was to blend in as best I could. I worked hard at it. Now, whether or not I did that proficiently is another question. However, I did learn how to play golf and hunt with some sort of proficiency—to be "one of the guys"—although I would've always preferred to stay back and make breakfast with my grandpa. To this day, I'd put my skillet gravy up against anyone's, thanks to the tutelage of Bill James. Don't play with a Texan and his gravy. (If you're taking notes, go ahead and jot that one down.) Gravy aside, my efforts to blend in where I was didn't come without a cost. For every action that felt artificial or untrue leaving my person, I felt myself withdraw from connection—first from my family, then from anyone who made me feel like I had to change my personality or passions to be loved . . . as if that pulling away would somehow protect who I really was.

It didn't take long to turn this childhood angst into isolation as I retreated further and further into myself. I focused on figuring out why I didn't fit in with much of the world around me and asked myself who I really was—*a lot*. Then, somehow, I began believing it was my family's responsibility to learn how to communicate with me on my terms.

I was a musical theater kid who wanted to be on Broadway as soon as possible (in between designing new roller coasters and attractions for Disney World, mind you). I was singularly focused on my interests and goals, and as a result, I maneuvered selfishly. I began expecting conversations to focus on what I wanted to talk about, and if they didn't, I disengaged. In my longing to be heard, I isolated myself from the very people I loved—and who loved me—the most. I was striking out on the self-awareness front because I didn't know I was an unappealing conversationalist—self-absorbed, even. Now, we'll discuss this more as we move on, but to quickly differentiate the two: self-awareness is an understanding of how you—what you're saying, how you're being, and what you're calling attention to—are received by or affect others. Self-absorption is when you're only focused on you, what you're saying, how you're being, and what you're calling attention to, others be damned.

It wouldn't be until I graduated high school that I realized the gap I forged between myself and my family was created by selfishness, my own self-absorption. Mine, not theirs. I had grown so consumed with my own thoughts, perspectives, and hurts that it was like I was breathing out carbon dioxide only to inhale it again—I was in my own bubble, like some astronaut whose suit was running out of oxygen. I wanted my loved ones to adjust to me because I was unique, talented in my way, and clearly figuring out who I was, but what I didn't appreciate at the time was that they were unique and talented, too. They were also figuring out who they were. Was I expecting them to do something—reach out and get to know me for *me*—I wasn't willing to do myself? Eventually,

I came to understand that I was, but that understanding would take years and a lot of work.

This isn't anything unusual. We all grow up and leave home after high school, or at some point, on a quest to figure out who we are. It's natural and necessary, and with it comes a certain degree of self-focus. It just comes with the territory. We each have that need to prioritize figuring out who we are, our chosen trajectory, and how we'll achieve the things we want in life. It's a needed component of our transformation from adolescent to adult. It's nothing to be ashamed of, but, at the same time, it is something to be left behind, little by little, as best we can.

What I've come to believe is that the less secure and accepting of ourselves we are, the more selfish we tend to stay. If I'm so consumed with how I'm not fitting in where I am, what could be different about me, how I'm coming across, what others are or aren't doing—I miss a huge piece of the relational puzzle: my contribution to the relationship. This can show up in a lot of different ways. We might play the victim or be the victimizer, or come across as confident and competitive or as self-absorbed. We can try to be macho or sexy to get validation from others. We can be loud and bombastic to try to distract from what is most sensitive in us. In short, we try to manipulate the world around us to look "right" on the outside so that we feel better on the inside. It's an attempt at building a route to another, but it's wrongly motivated and so wrongly received and felt. We want authentic connection, but we're misguided about how to get there.

Because all of us have tried to connect with someone through inauthentic means at some point, this tendency isn't anything to be ashamed of—understanding it is just part of the process. Just like no one should be surprised a six-year-old isn't five feet tall yet, no one in their twenties or thirties should be surprised they still have a lot to learn about being fully mature. We're all a work in progress and need the humility to embrace that. Those who don't embrace their own humility find themselves further than they'd like from a healthy relational partner—be it friend, romance, or business.

When we make so much of our lives about ourselves, we create circular thinking and justify our bad actions to ourselves. Our own spin (perspective) of a given situation takes up our mental real estate, which can cause us to become equally more "justified" in our minds and more isolated in our lives from healthy relational dynamics. This same thinking is what led me toward self-destruction in every way. It was rampant in the way I spoke, in how I made decisions, in how I treated everyone around me. And the more I acted this way, the more I withdrew—raising the drawbridge and yelling from the turret, "Scale the wall if you really care about seeing me."

While graduating high school, I found myself isolated from friends, family, and, honestly, anything truly good in my life—symbiotic relationships, community, being known in general, and knowing the gold there is in others. Selfishness has harmful ramifications if given free rein, and I was living it out loud. I had thought the only way to get what I needed was to fight for it at every turn, but that only made things worse. In choosing to fight for what I wanted, I always lost something—usually a relationship or two. Now, I still fight, but with different tools, a different motivation, and in the name of true connection rather than self-absorbed isolation. When I am fighting *for* people, instead of against them in the name of my own interests, I gain so much more.

You can tell where one's priorities are, what they're really fighting for, when you listen to the questions they ask in conversations. For instance, have you ever started chatting with someone and found yourself asking questions you really wish the other person was asking you so that you could talk about yourself? I used to be an expert at this approach. Ah, my early twenties. (Currently shaking my head in disbelief at myself here.) I was so good at talking with other people—*about myself.*

I'm not exactly sure when the lights came on for me, but maybe it was after a series of conversations during which I saw the lights go out for the people with whom I was speaking. It was like they shut down more and more as I kept trying to be center stage, and eventually they would make an excuse to leave or, worse, they would just endure it. I realized my strategy for living a full life had been backward. At some point, it was like a small person behind their eyeballs pulled down the shades, turned off the lights, and went to bed. They were checked out, and I just kept talking, totally self-absorbed.

I liked talking about myself way more than I cared about what other people had to say. That's no fun to admit, is it? But when I think about how many times I've asked a friend how they're doing with more excitement about giving my own answer than hearing theirs—*Cringe City.*

The fact is if I allow my own need for validation—to be heard and seen by others—to always upstage whomever I'm with, the result is always less than optimal. I'm denying myself the opportunity to really get to know someone and denying their opportunity to be known for who they are (and ironically, I'm keeping them from really getting to know me). By prioritizing what I thought was important, being seen as valuable by way of being funny or entertaining, I turned other people into contestants for attention to compete with rather than teammates with whom to dream and move forward.

Luckily, though, as the metaphorical lights went out for one more person I was talking at, I remembered my playground conversations with Ms. Prego and how they made me feel—seen, understood, and cared for. I began to realize that was *not* how I was making others feel as I droned on about myself. Sure, Ms. Prego shared personal stories, but as I thought back to our recess conversations, I began to realize every story she shared was simply a touch point to bring out more of me. She made me feel comfortable so that I could share my dreams with her, and in that way she validated them and encouraged me. I'll never forget her for that. As I traced her influence through my life to that point, I was able to recognize that so many other people—my precious parents, for starters—had been echoing a similar song to me, only I hadn't been open to hearing it sung by *them*.

However, as I began transitioning into adulthood, I began thinking it might be nice not to be forgotten either—to have a lasting impact on others by trying to see them for who they are and leaving them fuller and more encouraged than before. It might be nice to impart a portion of the kindness and curiosity that was invested in me, though it felt dormant at that moment. But no one could or would make the decision to shift my mindset for me. Was I going to get out of myself and into the world of people around me, or insist on building and living in my own snow globe, in the room but completely separate from it? That was no good.

So I decided to change the conversation and see my motivation in these conversations differently. Instead of asking leading questions that would create a chance for me to talk about myself, I started setting the stage so that I could hear about the dreams the other person had, or what they were really struggling to work through. I started listening to see who I might know who could help them to their next step or what I could do to make their aspirations more concrete. And as I did that, as I leaned out of myself and into the well-being of others, they became genuinely interested in my dreams and aspirations as well.

Suddenly, instead of pulling down the shades and turning out the lights, the little person behind their eyes was sitting with their elbows on the windowsill, fascinated to hear what I would say next. I have to admit, that really changed my perspective. And it also really changed how I saw people succeed in little ways around me. It felt as if they started inching closer to their dreams, day by day and conversation by conversation. I realized that we can have a tangible impact on others—and others can have a tangible impact on us—as soon as we look outward, apply some empathy, and get active. Our success and well-being are intertwined.

So, more and more, instead of expecting others to make room for me and to meet me on my terms, I decided to risk reaching out to them and trying to help them come out of their fortresses of solitude. I needed to get to know them well enough to figure out what they were good at and help them use it to connect with others. I was going to love them where they were and into wherever they wanted to go. I was going to be aware enough not to miss the important stuff, the small things many might look past or not see altogether.

I may have realized my relational tools were a bit sparse in high school, but it wasn't until I went to university that I began using each environment I was in as a testing ground to workshop the tools and principles I'm overjoyed to share with you now. Leaning out is key. I needed to forget about myself for a bit—what you might call "being more selfless"—and pay attention to what was going on with those around me to pull out the specific beauty I was now able to see in others.

By leaning out of myself, I learned to effectively invest in, develop, and support the health of different environments and the people in them. Even better, this "selfless awareness" of others established a new "true north" for every conversation I had or conflict I helped resolve—meaning that regardless of blips of selfishness or mistakes made in behavior, once we decide on our mode of selflessly being aware, we will consistently find ourselves pointed "north" in our actions and relationships as a whole.

Let's take a moment to further define "selfless awareness" and "true north" as I use them in this book. Selfless awareness is an awareness of those immediately around you and is untethered to you and your motives, wants, or priorities. It's an ability to be in an environment and astute to the needs, wants, and "temperature" of the overall atmosphere, unencumbered by your own agenda.

A "true north" here is your established way of being. It doesn't mean you don't deviate from it, but it means that regardless of the deviation, your orientation is "north." I love to help meet immediate needs; it's a "true north" quality I have prioritized. However, there are days and moments when I'm less able or inclined to help meet each immediate need I see. That doesn't change my intent as a person. So in my maturing I had to set a new "north" because my old compass of behavior was oriented to prioritize me and my goals, wants, and interests above all else. Instead of living in a way that takes or detracts from a setting, I shifted my attention to pouring into and serving others more than not—being an addition. As I leaned out of myself and helped others make room to also lean out, I discovered I was getting healthier and inching toward the kind of life I really wanted. I was exercising real relational muscles in the world, which was replenishing who I was and who I was becoming.

I began to understand what Stephen Covey meant when he talked about "Emotional Bank Accounts." As he put in his famous book, *The 7 Habits of Highly Effective People*,

> If I make deposits into an Emotional Bank Account with you through courtesy, kindness, honesty, and keeping my commitments to you, I build a reserve. Your trust toward me becomes higher and I can call upon that trust many times if I need to . . .
>
> But if I have a habit of showing discourtesy, disrespect, cutting you off, overreacting, ignoring you, becoming arbitrary, betraying your trust, threatening you, or playing little tin god in your life, eventually my Emotional Bank Account is overdrawn. The trust level gets very low. Then what flexibility do I have?*

In my own mind, I began to add to this metaphor. I saw the "Emotional Bank Accounts" Covey mentions more like an investment portfolio of people. I began to think of "investing" in others in terms of building "equity"—equity is the difference between what you owe and what assets you have growing in your portfolio—in their lives and in our relationship. The more I am able to invest in others, the healthier their relational balance sheet becomes, and the more they have to invest in others (and sometimes I'm one of those others!).

Building Relational Equity

When the COVID-19 pandemic swept the globe, I fell into an interesting situation. I was in Los Angeles when the first lockdown hit, on what was supposed to be just a fun weekend visiting one of my closest friends, his wife who has also become one of my closest,

* Stephen R. Covey, *The 7 Habits of Highly Effective People: Powerful Lessons in Personal Change* (New York: Fireside, 1989), 188.

and a number of creative types ranging from close friends to acquaintances. Finding ourselves suddenly unable to travel, our hosts invited us to stay put and quarantine with them until the "shelter in place" mandate was lifted. There we were, a collection of eleven people, acquaintances, friends, and "personalities" living together for what ended up being nearly three months. It was a full house. You probably couldn't have collected a more diverse group if you'd tried.

We were filmmakers, painters, musicians, writers, and A-list entertainers. We were from different backgrounds, geographies, and political viewpoints. Throw into the mix that our group represented about five different faith belief systems, and you begin to see just how potentially dynamic our environment was.

Yet what might have been disastrous turned into a beautiful workshop in the power of building relational equity. Every day we had to "read the room" anew. There were some big personalities among us and little personal space. Many situations could have turned into major clashes, and hard conversations were definitely had. But because of the relational equity we built with each other each day through genuine and full-hearted conversations, attuning ourselves to see and sense each other's real needs, putting our hands to work where we could as a team, and pouring empathy over it all—there was an abundance of grace extended to one another, and you could feel the thankfulness with which we each received it.

And then it got interesting.

Parked in one place together like that, we talked to each other—a lot. As that happened, we discussed dreams and ideas. Next career or life steps and new projects were discussed, and since we had nothing but time, we started contributing to each other—investing not only in our conversations and relationships, but in our actual futures and successes, too. Songs were written and the music was beautiful. Film and television treatments got fleshed out, connections were made, Zoom readings took place, and in the end—real and legitimate business was done. Like kids in some old 1930s comedy, we pulled out trunks of old clothes and put on our own shows, with each other as our audience. Being "stuck together" turned into a time I was sorry to see end. Don't get me wrong. We were each very grateful, as I'm certain our loving hosts were, that life was going back to "normal." But what we experienced in our once-in-a-lifetime bubble was pretty remarkable, if you ask me. The day I finally left to return home felt like the end of summer camp.

But all of that collaboration and relationship building didn't just *happen*. We had to work at it. What I had learned about building relational equity, and the choices we made every day in our pursuit of loving each other genuinely made a difference for our group altogether. I began to implement many of the selflessly aware strategies I'm going to outline for you. We each knew that our thriving through that time was dependent on our tangible investment. And like an orchestra tuning, we saw each other pick up our bows, reeds, and instruments and began hearing each other, tuning ourselves to work together in harmony, not in dissonance and out of pitch. In doing so, I found great joy in being my own Swiss Army knife of empathy and helpfulness for everyone there, doing what I could to help create an environment of trust and increase our collective relational equity. Now, did I hit that out of the park each day? In no way.

However, as we begin to have this conversation of holistic relational health, of understanding and interpreting what we see, of meeting others from the healthiest, most purely motivated place—there are a few ways we can begin to shift our mindset.

The following are some simple ways to build relational equity right where you are.

Lean out of yourself and into others.
While I've already discussed this at length above, creating relational equity begins in the most basic of interactions: in conversation and in how it feels to be in another's presence. When we sincerely listen and are selflessly aware of the needs of others, it lays the foundation for more positive conversations and interactions in the future. It allows people to relax and feel comfortable, and lets them know the environment is a safe place to try out new things. This makes room for empathy to do its work and tears down barriers in amazing ways.

Start something or join in.
Is someone starting dinner? Offer to slice up the onion or to wash dirty cookware as the need arises. (An offer, I can guarantee you, no one will turn down.) Is someone straightening up? Jump in to help. Does anyone want to play a game? Help set up the board and grab a scorecard. Someone putting in a movie? Make popcorn and see if people want something to sip on. Time for a sing-along? Grab your guitar (or a tambourine, if that's more your speed). Are you the first one up in the morning? Learn the coffee preferences of your people and play barista.

At your workplace, is there a way you can jump-start productive conversation by introducing an item from the news relevant to your industry during Monday meetings? It may spark some curiosity and start to reengage settled professionals into new growth in their roles. Or maybe you want to change the tone of how coworkers speak to each other. If your workplace has been a place where compliments and qualities "worth celebrating" are often unnoticed, begin to shift that culture by thoughtfully and intentionally shining a light on a person and a quality worth shouting out.

Energy multiplies when someone seconds your idea and immediately jumps in to help make it happen. Then, by the time you have three people on board, fun is virtually guaranteed. There's nothing worse than an "I don't wanna" attitude that sucks the oxygen out of a room. Besides, you can only sit and do nothing for so long. Live a little! If you need, just pump up "Scrubbing Day" from the seminal 1988 classic *The New Adventures of Pippi Longstocking*. It works on a solid 60 percent of millennials. And yes, I support this being played in offices as well. Don't @ me.

Set the conditions for success.

Environment matters. With a lot of people in one space, it's easy for things to get cluttered, and the messier things are, the less patience people have for one another. And the easiest time to clean up is when the mess is small. Someone forgot to take their plate to the kitchen? Pick it up, give it a quick rinse, and stick it in the dishwasher. Done. The dishwasher's full? Unload it. (It takes about five minutes, believe me—I've timed it!) Trash can full? Empty it. People a little grumpy after dinner? Make cleanup as fun as you can—turn it into a singalong or switch chores around. Maybe even have a few "Would You Rather" questions to start fun conversation flowing. Time to chill? Put on some good music. Time to party? Right! Put on some good music at a respectable level and watch people breathe a little easier.

If your work has a competitive atmosphere, be excited about others' wins and even help them accomplish their goals as much as you can within your role. It isn't costly to encourage someone, to take an extra glance at a report, to give a little insight where you have it. These little investments yield big atmospheric wins.

You get the idea. Be constantly thinking of how you can set the stage for success.

Do the little things you can do.

Never underestimate the power of little things. Skip that second latte a day, invest the money in an account, and you'll be surprised how quickly it grows. In the same way, little investments of trust, positivity, kindness, encouragement, doing what you said you would do, and the like add up quickly. This sort of investment is accrued cumulatively and with consistency.

Is the kitchen in your office a little unkempt? Remind yourself to wipe down the counters at the end of the day, a couple times a week. Is there a new person in your office? Reach out to invite them to lunch. Did you take notes for yourself in a meeting? Share them with your coworkers afterward.

Be willing to honestly say "no."

You're an agent of awareness, thoughtfulness, and action. However, you're not a doormat. Different people react differently when you offer to do things for them, when you lean out of yourself. Some will chip in and join you; others are glad to let you do all the work and avoid the unpleasant tasks. Together always feels better than "Let me get that for you." Know your limits and when you're better off doing something in a different room or giving yourself some private time. More than that, knowing what you're able and unable to do will keep you from overcommitting yourself. Although we want to show up in the ways we're meant to, we don't want to show up depleted because of the pressure we put on ourselves or the pressure we feel from others. So know how to feel perfectly free to say an unemotional and light "No." Or even, "Thank you for thinking of me, but no. I'm unable to do that." I promise the quicker you incorporate that short sentiment, in all its iterations, the freer you'll be to give of yourself where you're meant to.

Those are just a few ways to build relational equity in any environment, but they make a great start for where we're headed.

Over the weeks our shelter-in-place group was together, we stretched ourselves to meet each other with real empathy, and we thrived. Not one of us was the center of our own world, which led to us functioning as a real and potent community. Truthfully, life in general works best when we're not the axis on which it spins.

Of course, you don't have to be living in a house with ten other people to practice building relational equity. Wherever people are, there will also be a way to create more equity or to deplete it. Taking an extra couple of minutes to check in on a coworker when you don't have to? Investment. Not following through with something you said you were going to do? Withdrawal. Connecting a friend with someone else you respect just because? Investment. Being unaware while at a friend's house and not engaging in conversation with others there? Withdrawal.

Do you notice if your barista is having a crummy day? Even more importantly, if you noticed, would it affect your interaction? We often underestimate the importance of how we engage with others, even in the smallest of encounters.

Relational Agency

In the same way that using a consistent set of principles and techniques in construction makes for a more stable and effective structure, I use what I've learned to practice building healthy relationships and encourage creative environments. But the key is that I actually practice; I actually use my choice in the matter to move the rest of me (motivation and action) into alignment with my desire to have a stable and life-giving relational world. Like ingesting nutritious foods and exercising contributes to a healthy lifestyle, time and again I have seen the principles we'll uncover in this book lead to healthy relationships and blossoming careers. You might think of it like finding a delicious new cookbook—it's just the beginning of tasty new dishes and memorable evenings.

When you listen to genuinely hear someone, you build camaraderie and trust, which are helpful in many situations. When you're aware of how you come across in conversation, you minimize disconnections (the moments when that small person on the other side of their eyes pulls the shades and beds down for the night). When you understand how to contextually let body language, even at a very surface level, clue you in, you become astute and sensitive to the unspoken emotions and feelings of others. When you know what you're willing and able to contribute, you don't extend yourself beyond what your capabilities or person allow. Knowing someone else and being able to meet them exactly where they are fills relationships with potential energy—who knows what incredible things might come of your collaborations simply because you made a new connection?

This isn't empty idealism. I've seen what knowing someone and meeting them where they are can accomplish. But it's not something you can do once and expect a relationship to blossom with wonder. Rather, this practice of leaning out of yourself and into others needs to be developed into a rhythm of life you create with each new interaction with another person. It needs to become your new normal. You need to reset some of your defaults. We all do.

Slight adjustments can yield big results if applied consistently over time. In taking our eyes off ourselves in the daily, we will see a new world of opportunities around us. Not only will we start attracting and sustaining healthy relationships in our own lives, but we will also start planting seeds of health and wonder into the lives of others. Like planting trees will eventually provide life to the ground and air around them, selfless investment of other-centered awareness yields enormous and environmental rewards. When we invest in people with their best interests in mind, we create a fortress of friendship, support, and safety—allies of deep relationships we can run to and rest in throughout our lives.

About a year ago, I began working with a young woman who represents this principle perfectly. She's someone who has survived a barrage of hard and disorienting life events that would turn anyone on their head. In our first meeting, as we began walking through the dynamics of the relationships and friendships in her life, one thing became abundantly clear: she didn't know she could decide the kind of relationships she had with others.

She expressed a significant amount of shame, manipulation, and control she felt from a slew of people entrenched in her life. I listened to her communicate an opinion of herself that sounded like a distorted echo of the influences surrounding her. These relationships were bankrupting all the relational equity she had stored, leaving her with none to invest in return.

The truth is, she didn't know she had the right to set a new rhythm for how her relationships functioned. She didn't know that she had the right to learn and glean from those she respected and to respectfully disregard the thoughts of those whose intentions she didn't trust. But what I know, and what she now knows, is that we get to decide who does and does not speak into our lives. When it comes down to it, we want to "do life" with those who know how to invest in others and understand what it takes to make us feel loved, seen, and valued. We want to do life with those who are interested in developing relational equity with us—not those looking to make as large a withdrawal as possible.

Regardless of how we're raised, regardless of what seemed normal growing up, we get to choose the amount of health and functionality we have in our relationships and in our life. I have loved watching her as she dives headfirst into recalibrating the way she sees herself, what she's willing to give to and expect from relationships, and what boundaries she places to protect her heart and sanity. All I had to do was tell her she had permission to advocate for healthier dynamics in her life. It was something she never realized before. She thought she had to react to everyone around her, for better or for worse. She didn't realize she could respond instead with, "Yes, that, but no, not that."

Now when I see her, I am greeted with the beautiful and quiet confidence she has developed but may not even see herself yet. I've had a blast watching her life fill with opportunities she would have let someone tell her she didn't deserve before. She has started to fill her life with people genuinely invested in her well-being.

And that's what creating relational equity is all about, but first things first. Before we move on to the next chapter, I'd like to acquaint you with how I'll end each chapter, so you have a real sense of where I'm meaning to lead us. Now, as much as I enjoy a passive reading experience and way to escape, this isn't that. We can discuss principles all day long, but until you put your hands on them and pull them into your reality, they mean nothing. You can't truly master another language by reading textbooks alone or hearing it and never speaking it yourself. Instead, you have to stumble through its vernacular and pronunciation as it comes out of your own mouth, learning its appropriate usages and how to bring every bit of yourself to the language.

PUTTING IT INTO PRACTICE: Little Leans

So now, an invitation. At the end of each chapter, I'm going to give you a list of opportunities and ways to employ some of the principles we've just discussed. Pick two to three to test out while in your daily ventures and notice how you feel afterward. As we move through the book, the opportunities will shift and grow in nature. But for now, let's start with these *little leans*, or small ways to engage with others:

- Call a friend and ask about a specific part of their life. Choose to care about the answers you get and allow the conversation to stay centered on them as long as you're able. The point is to get comfortable engaging someone where they are, and to meet them with curiosity in the way they need that day.
- Take notice of a specific coffee/tea/water preference of a coworker. If it's unclear, ask. "Now, do you enjoy a green tea every morning or were you just feeling that today?" Next time you pick up a morning beverage, bring one of their favs. For bonus points, let it be someone you're not already close to.
- As you approach a checkout line and find someone else walking toward the same line, simply slow your pace, smile with eye contact if possible, and give way to the other person to go first. Yes, I know this sounds basic and you might not even be acknowledged for your

small and selfless action. Go ahead and get used to that now.

- Say something kind to a stranger while out and about. Now, let's not be creepy and compliment physicality, but instead look for something beyond appearance. If you hear someone say something funny, laugh and say something like, "Thank you for that. I needed a laugh today." One of my personal favorites is to compliment a parent out and about with their kids, especially if they are palpably overwhelmed: "Hey, well done, parent." It doesn't need to be deep; it just needs to be a pleasant and kind exchange prompted by you.

These little leans will begin to change how and what you see in the world around you. One of the first things you'll begin to notice are the very tangible gaps of understanding, connectedness, and empathy often present in all of us.

2

Mind the Gap

DISTANCE IS SOMETHING INHERENT IN any relationship. This distance could be physical, say when you and a friend or partner live across the country from one another. Or it could be emotional, like when you and a coworker keep butting heads when working on a project and you aren't sure why. Regardless of the reason for the distance, being mindful of that space between us as individual people can be the beginning of cultivating real emotional awareness of others. If that seems unsettling to you at first, you're not alone. And although physical distance can have a major impact on our relationships, in this chapter I'd like to focus on emotional, or relational, distance. Have a fight with your spouse you leave unresolved? That's a distance creator over time. Have you ever gone to another country and tried speaking with someone only to discover a language barrier between you? Distance. Those might be obvious examples. So now let's think about situations we all encounter but might not recognize. Think about starting a job at a new workplace with its own social rules, hierarchy, and culture.

There's a starting distance between you and your coworkers, not an irreconcilable distance, but distance—a gap. Think about dating a new person. Even though there might be excitement and anticipation for the future, there is also a tremendous amount of distance to bridge before you can really connect.

I love how concerned with this gap the United Kingdom is. You quite literally see "Mind the Gap" on signs throughout the Underground stations and other public places. "Minding the Gap" in London, for instance, means being aware of your spatial surroundings in public places and to "watch your step." This may mean to watch the space between a train and platform or bus and sidewalk, but also to watch your space in conjunction with people around you. It is a social rule to be understood and respected, and, honestly, I'm a big fan of it. I remember visiting the United Kingdom as a child and not understanding this phrase. However, I do remember observing how it was taken to heart. If there is space in a line, you can count on someone to fill it. If you are too close to someone, it's expected that you back up and give them a bit of room. In general, "minding the gap" means watching your surroundings and adjusting your actions to what is best and safest for the entire group—not just you. A large city housing millions of people means there are millions of different agendas, dreams, personalities, cultural backgrounds, understandings, traumas, and life-wins. For one to not only survive but thrive in an incredibly diverse environment like this, there is a need and expectation to put "self" on the back burner long enough to be present where you are with those around you, even if that's a bus stop.

Interestingly, if you've spent time in other big cities, you might also observe a different expression of the same sentiment: be aware of where you are. If you're in New York City, you might not hear

"Mind the Gap," but you could possibly hear a slew of expletives telling you to move, watch where you're going, or simply to walk faster. If you ever see me walking like something's on fire, just know that I lived in New York in my early twenties and that pace just hasn't left me. Do my friends yell at me for walking too fast now? Yes, of course. In fact, this trait can even turn physical distance into relational distance. One time, I was walking with one of my closest friends talking about life and all of a sudden I realized she had stopped about two hundred feet behind me. She was just waiting to see if I would notice as I kept right on talking and walking. We had a laugh about it, but the reality was that I was in my own world, and I had exchanged my awareness of the person I was talking to for my desire to go at *my* pace. In this instance, it cost me some light chastising and a reality check. Likewise, my walking head up, gawking, in the middle of Times Square might cost me being called a name. My walking into oncoming traffic might cost me a hospital visit or possibly my life. There are real ramifications to our (lack of) awareness and how we steward the space between ourselves and the world around us.

When We Create Gaps

Every person is selfish in their own way, for their own reasons. And for us to advance, professionally or personally, we need to understand how our personal brand of selfishness drives our daily lives. If you're head-tilted right now, thinking, *I don't know about that*, let me ask you a question: Have you ever had to teach a child how to say "No," "I want," or "Not fair"? I doubt it. Chances are you've found what I have in each one of my incredible ten nieces and nephews:

We're already hardwired to look out for ourselves. This hardwiring is evident when we become aware of what we need in relation to our surroundings and what is essential for us to be able to advocate for ourselves. But when our self-advocacy forces us to choose between another person or group and their needs or our convenience or personal priorities, we arrive at a valuable crossroad.

Let's put this on its feet in a very practical and relatable way. Let's talk about food and kids' birthday parties. I remember being in elementary school at one of the endless strings of birthday parties and each time a box of pizza was brought out and opened, I would begin sizing up the piece(s) I wanted. Depending on the kind of pizza, I would assess the toppings allotment on each piece, size up the amount of real estate the crust was taking, and immediately have tiers 1, 2, and 3 options of preference. Now this by itself isn't necessarily bad, right? I had preferences and understood what factors contributed to what I considered to be a successful pizza score. But if you had been with me on a number of occasions when I was a child, you would see a visual grimace, definite shift in attitude, and an overall highly dramatized response if I didn't get the piece I wanted. It's not a cute look. Why? There are always more people at the table than me—at pizza parties and in life. I traded my enjoyment of the people around the table for a pseudo-victory in life. The pizza was there to feed me and my friends. Instead of being thankful for the gathering and the generosity, I made myself and a very minor facet of the whole reason I was there my primary focus. In hindsight, I probably made a scene, embarrassed my family, and created a level of awkwardness no one enjoys. I created a relational gap between myself and the other partygoers. Here in this little moment, my selfishness cost me and those around me enjoyment and ease . . . and that's just a pizza party.

Decisions we make don't exist in a vacuum and often carry a cost that we don't anticipate. It doesn't matter how innocuous our selfish moments seem; as we look at their effects in our lives, we begin to build a data set of actions/behaviors with corresponding responses/results. This might be easiest to see from another seat.

For us to truly get a personal look at this, think about an average day in your life. You might work from home or be a part of a large corporation; you may already be retired and in a different phase of life altogether. You might be in college right now trying to figure out your next step or possibly in the middle of starting your family. Who knows, you could be in any variation of these options and countless others. Regardless of what your day-to-day looks like, let me ask you this: Do people ever annoy you?

I doubt that's where you thought I was going, but here we are nonetheless. Of *course* people can be annoying. That's a fact of life right along with the sun coming up each day. The real question is, is savoring being annoyed worth the chasm it causes? In other words, what's more important to you, holding a grudge or having a relationship? Healthy boundaries are necessary. And sometimes your body sends you signals to warn you about an unhealthy interaction. But sometimes, we do need to dig deep and realize that *we* are the common denominator and have some work of our own to do. We have more agency than we may realize when it comes to navigating these relational gaps.

When Others Create Gaps

Up until this point we've discussed the cost of selfishness. If you have a partner in life who is only interested in talking about themselves, their wins and their losses, and what concerns them primarily, it's difficult to truly believe that they are interested in who you really are. If you have worked in unhealthy environments where you've seen ideas and credit hijacked by those in leadership, it genuinely affects your buy-in of that business, let alone your ability to thrive in that work culture. Selfish behaviors drain the oxygen out of whatever boardroom, living room, and relationship in which they're allowed to parade.

Now let's move away from whatever your office space looks like. Let's go play. Specifically, let's meet up at an amusement park. Now, I can't promise this will be the last time I reference amusement parks, so I'm not even going to pretend like it is. I love amusement parks because they strip away the camouflage that obscures some key human behaviors. For example, the way people navigate lines and queues is a master class in the way people think. I'll never forget being a plump, awkward preteen in line for a water ride . . . Yes, I said I was plump because I need you to understand my need to cool down was no joke. Let's move on.

Behind me, I hear a mother explaining to everyone she's practically elbowing past, "Oh, I'm so sorry . . . Yes, you see his brothers and sisters are up there and they've been waiting to ride together . . . Oh, I'm so sorry, my husband has been in line and my kiddo just had to go to the bathroom." I mean, she was doing real work to make sure we all understood she was perfectly fine to scootch past us toward the front. Now, allow me to quickly say that even then I didn't have a second thought about letting them by, nor did anyone else. ("Oh my gosh, of course" was the most common response.) After several minutes of watching this mother and child snake through the line, they arrived at their friend—not husband or father—at which point the mother immediately started laughing, saying, "Oh my gosh, people really believed me. You should've seen it." Mind you, we're all in a line that snakes back and forth and can hear her quite clearly.

I don't share this story to say, "Ooh, how bad of her. Isn't that selfish?" Honestly, I'd be surprised if anyone else from that line remembers this incident. But even as a child it made me sad because you could feel the palpable disengagement and distrust from those who had just witnessed what I had. More than that, you could see it on the face of the child who'd been used for line-advancement. The embarrassment with which he flushed at the lack of knowing or acknowledgment from the adults in his life. It was all there to plainly see. There was a relational withdrawal made with that one continued, intentional, selfish action. If you were to ask that mother what the cost of her manipulation was that day, she'd probably tell you there wasn't one. She might even say, "They were just some white lies, and after all, it was vacation, right?"

I'd argue the one who paid the highest price for that action was the child being used as a prop. I watched that small and confused face, learning and gleaning from what was being lived out and trying to understand it for himself. While he was making sense of what just happened, the two women laughed, completely unaware of the icky atmosphere they brought to a line of people who were patiently waiting to be drenched in theme-park water. A drop of selfishness changed the temperature of that water, and the ecosystem shifted in an instant.

Whatever modes and behaviors have been "successful" for a person become familiar and worn in like grooves on an LP, and those default behaviors become the drivers when a person disengages their selfless muscles and goes to the "just being" muscles they might've thought they earned to exercise during vacation.

If you're not sure what these "just being" muscles look like, I'll tell you. It's that mode you're in when you don't have to account for any bit of "I *should*." How do you clean your place when no one's coming over versus when you're having some of your favorite people for dinner? It's a slightly different thing, right? How do you take notes in a meeting for yourself compared to how you take notes for your employer when they ask? They might not be largely different approaches, but the intention is different enough to bring about marginal changes to the effort and focus made, and thus, the result is different.

Here's an example. I don't enjoy small talk. I realize this is a book about engaging beyond yourself, about knowing the life it brings to yours once you lean out. But it's hard for me, too, and I often have to check my own cruise control to make sure it's off. Even knowing how valuable small interactions can be doesn't keep my selfishness at bay, especially when I believe I'm in what I call a "public-private place."

Public-Private Place

That grocery store, vacation destination, airplane ride, large meeting, or giant party you think you can disappear in? You can't. These are innately public places, and while you may feel anonymous in a crowd, they're actually full of constant micro-interactions with other human beings. It's simultaneously intimate, private, and outward-facing, and your actions matter.

For nearly a year of my life, I drove back and forth between Los Angeles and Dallas on a monthly basis, as well as made a monthly road trip to Nashville for added kicks. If you're grimacing or possibly gagging at the thought, I understand that and feel you. It logistically made sense for a time, as crazy as that sounds, but it was a lot. However, this amount of travel time has given me a great deal of perspective on highways, which I think of as the epitome of the public-private place. Allow me to explain. *Cracks knuckles*

Turn signals. Flow of traffic. Left lane usage. Appropriate follow length. Pressing the brake versus stomping on it—there are a lot of little decisions happening in the public-private environment of being in one's car. Does it matter how I brake if I'm on a racetrack by myself? Well, it will matter to my brake pads, but that's about it. But I told you I drive a lot, right, and on roads with a lot of people? So let's combine my braking habits with someone who is a little quick on the gas pedal. This results in a gap to be bridged: my individual driving habits with that of a roadway full of other drivers. Now let's say we're in the middle of construction or slow-moving traffic. Nothing bad can happen when two drivers "just being" meet on the road, right?

I like to slow down when and how I want. You like to speed up when and how you want. But regardless of where the law might place the blame, if we collide, we've both contributed to the circumstances allowing that collision. Why? Because beyond our own ways of existing are others and their ways of existing—a gap between our functioning and the world around us. Not only do we need to steward what's in our hands (the ways we speak to others, decisions we make, and choices in operation); we have to steward those things in the context of a world not based on ourselves. *That's* the relational gap for us to mind.

Let's meet up at whatever meeting place or boardroom feels most comfortable for you. Hypothetically, you've just finished a massive project with a team of five. You all felt the work distribution to be fair, that everyone contributed what they ought to have contributed, and there really weren't any big issues. Wonderful, that's a massive equity win for everyone at the table. You've all grown respect, trust, belief, and overall camaraderie as a team. There aren't gaps of understanding or teamwork, workload imbalances, or lack of ability. You genuinely felt like you all functioned together effectively.

Now immediately after this project is finished you go to present it to your employers. You and each member of your team have talked through what portion of this presentation they'll give with highlighted takeaways, wins, and truth bombs to be dispersed with design. The meeting starts and you, along with your coworkers, get up to present. As Miriam begins speaking and talking through her section of the presentation, she gets to an especially important fact. She highlights it, but your coworker Paul is immediately dissatisfied with the attention it got so he chimes in—"Actually, it's not that it's *difficult* to make deliveries on time with that lead, it's impossible. Also, something else to note is ________." He might as well have said, à la Kanye, "I'mma let you finish, but . . ."

Now, of course, this doesn't upset a whole presentation and it's not something that would most likely even be talked about after. In the real world, this presentation may have been exactly what was being asked. Paul showed himself to be passionate in a moment, but who knows how that was perceived, right? Once words leave our mouth or a decision has been made, it's not up to us how it's received or felt. Paul made a shortsighted decision and his win in this scenario is no different.

Being a part of a team, even on a project, means that there are more people at the table than you. And when one part of a team chooses their win over the collective win, it's the equivalent of being at that pizza party again watching the chosen pieces be claimed without regard. You might get what you want, but you've also gotten a lot more of what you don't want—less relational equity and a greater relational gap.

In Paul's case, he might've left that meeting feeling like what he said was incredibly important and needed in the moment. Sure, he may get some adulation with the group for the presentation; he might possibly get an extra "We really appreciate your care," but truthfully Paul's losses here are far more than his gains. Walking out with his shoulders back, he might be unaware of the side-eyes two of his coworkers are giving each other. He might not even be aware that his teammate, Miriam, was going to reiterate the same point at the end of her section of the presentation and that he cut her off. He's probably not aware of the tangible awkwardness he created in the room when he spoke out. And whether or not he realized it, his priority hadn't actually been the team; it had been *his* win. He got his piece of pizza this time. Before too long, however, he might not be invited back to the party. Paul created distance between himself and his coworkers in that presentation—a true gap. Where once they may have been aligned by the same vision and requirements, they now know Paul will try to pull out in front of the pack when possible. Of course, these revelations are mostly unspoken because people don't usually feel the need to address what they feel they've already figured out.

There are environments that reward selfishness, and metrics and business structures that reward hogging the credit and alienating team members. But there are ways to pull ahead, to shine and to win, without costing the goodwill of colleagues and sacrificing relational equity along the way. You can summit the mountain without leaving the bodies of your teammates along the trail. You are making your path rockier and steeper than it needs to be when you have to fight outside elements and your own teammates at the same time. You can switch teams, replace team members, and change course—all while remaining on good terms. Just think, each teammate has skills that you have no idea they possess. They might not be the exact skills you need now. But you don't really know what they can do with their potential. What skills will they develop in the future? What relationships will they forge? You don't know for sure. So even if you have to share difficult truths with them or remove them from your team, if you deposit relational equity now, imagine the choices you'll have in the future. Every person you work with could be on your future team. Their relationships could become your relationships. Their skills could be applied to what you need. Your destiny might be impacted by their future. Don't let your selfish impulses overshadow the humanity of your team.

We can do better. But how? We can start by cultivating an awareness of how we show up in relationships and how we contribute to our relational environments. It's about understanding the ramifications of our actions and words. With each decision to live more selflessly, we align ourselves with a life associated with that selflessness: genuine two-sided relationships, upward momentum in vocations, and a more fulfilling relational world.

Healthy behaviors, leaning out to others, lead to closing gaps. We get to choose how we show up in the world, so why not choose to show up in a way that brings us closer to each other and to our purpose?

Set the Table

I love cooking, especially for people I love. It's something I learned from my mother, as she can truly do anything in the kitchen. Beyond that, she is a host at the highest level. She's exceptional at making people feel welcome and perfectly accepted as they are, a truly beautiful gift. It's one of the many qualities I admire about her, and one I've tried to emulate. Whether or not she knows it, she leaves no gap between herself and those welcomed to her home, taking every opportunity to add value to her environment and care to others by way of her tangible kindness. However, I've learned something about hosting and myself: When I'm stressed, my guests are stressed. In such situations, the gap is between my guests and me, and our ability to be at ease with each other. My intention to host well and create a nice atmosphere doesn't matter. If I'm running all over the place, flinging oven doors shut in between washing a dish and making a pesto, then I can tangibly feel the overall heart rate in the room rise with mine. That gap between us and our good time grows. It begins to feel stressful and my anxiety "sets the table" for the evening, prying open a certain amount of distance between me and my guests.

In the same way, how we move throughout the world sets the table for each interaction we have. Have you ever had a friend (or maybe it's been you—it's definitely been me) who talks about wanting a romantic relationship but seems so unapproachable? If you want to meet someone out and about, you should probably open your eyes and not look down, maybe wear an outfit you feel comfortable and confident in, and be kind . . . right? Just for starters. The gap between singleness and partnership is one that has to be bridged, too. Wearing sunglasses inside, AirPods in, and checking your feed while you're waiting in line just doesn't say, "Hey, I'd love to chat about the weather with you and then maybe grab coffee and hang out forever." So instead of being mad at the existing gap between you and a potential new relationship, there are some simple things you can do to set the table for what you're wanting to experience . . . to bridge a gap. It might be getting into therapy so you can be the healthiest version of you, it could be taking better care of yourself in general, it could be telling your friends you're open to meeting people (parameters included, of course; let's not get crazy).

This doesn't just apply to dating. Every environment offers us the opportunity to set the table now for the results we'd like to see in the future. Have you ever overheard the way someone condescendingly communicates to their loved one in their own public-private space and thought, *Oh, they must be a real* treat *to be married to.* Now imagine you see that person the next day as you start your new job and find out they're your manager. How excited would you be about this new relationship? Maybe less than over the moon, I'm supposing. That peek into their private life colored your experience of them in their professional life.

Obviously not each person we engage with on a passing level is someone we see down the road, but if I've learned anything, it's that you can't take back first impressions—even when you don't know you're giving one. This is not to lay undue burden on you, because we can't live as if each interaction carries the same weight, because they just don't. However, when we operate from a place of unawareness, thinking our passing exchanges and how we exist in context to others doesn't matter much, we lop off a portion of opportunity. It's like living off a limited lunch menu without realizing you have access to a whole kitchen and every kind of deliciousness available. Minding the distance between you and your immediate world puts you in a position to win relationally—everywhere.

Since observation is a key component here, I'd like for you to simply take notice of the people you respect most in your life. I'm not talking about respect based on obligation or your perceptions of monetary or vocational success. Think about the solid individuals you can proverbially hang a hat on, the ones you see as autonomous and healthy adults. We communicate much about ourselves without ever opening our mouths, and I'd argue that the people you respect most carry a piece of what they're looking for in others into each room they enter. No, this doesn't mean finding versions of ourselves to link arms with, but we do want to find recognizable healthy traits in those around us. We attract what we put out into the world, so we ought to be aware of what we're attracting.

So, in the ways we're able, with the tools we have, we look for and gravitate toward those we feel we can trust based on what we're allowed to see. Adjusting the ways we communicate and bridging interpersonal gaps can kick-start the metabolism of our selflessness. This happens verbally, yes, but nonverbally as well.

Up until this point, you might not have realized how much distance is up for grabs in life, relationally, vocationally, and socially. Gaps everywhere. If you can bridge them, you move closer to everything you've ever wanted. Now that you can see them, are you content with the gap between you and the relational world that sets you up for long-term wins? Let's mind it together, shall we? Here are a few of my favorite quick gap-menders:

- If you sense someone you love deep in thought, or possibly ruminating on a mistake made, take a moment and affirm/shout out what you know to be true (and opposite of what they're telling themselves). If your spouse is one to take on more than their share at work, you might say, "Honey, I'm so proud of how hard you work. I know you always give it your best and that makes me so proud."
- When you can sense someone's stress or time-crunched schedule at the supermarket (or airport, store, car mechanic, and so on), offer to let them go in front of you in line.
- When you encounter someone in customer service who is clearly irritated, take a moment from whatever exchange you're having and say, "Hey, how are you doing?" This

may catch them off guard, but stay engaged and genuinely inquire about his or her day. They may stay irritated, and that's okay. You stay kind and then move on with the transaction/interaction. You don't need to tell them they seemed irritated. Just be an immovable kindness for a moment and see what it does.

- When you have a careless moment, don't be afraid to laugh at it and call it out. Humility endears.
- Give a specific compliment to a coworker when you sense that they are overwhelmed, especially within earshot of others.
- Meet a simple and immediate need where you see it. Refill someone's water bottle, grab a coffee, or some other small gesture.

This is just a list to prime your imagination, because only *you* know what those in your environments truly need and the gaps that are present, so use your context.

From Here to There

If I think about where I want to be toward the end of my life and where I am now, I come into contact with a truth: there is a very real distance between these two points. It feels like a great distance from here to *there.* You might be thinking, "My savings account isn't quite yet stacked the way I'd like it to be; I haven't bought that dream property I've picked out for myself; my family unit isn't established; and I'm still a long way off from that rocking chair and wraparound porch I plan to have." I have gaps in my own life. That rocking chair, surrounded by my future family, is in my distance, too. Am I made for rocking chair commentary? Yes. But I know I have work to do before I get there.

Gaps exist everywhere and in specifically unique ways.

Do you ever think about the distance between you and the world around you? Speaking as someone who grew up in the buckle of the Bible Belt as a very extroverted, animated, and gregarious guy . . . I know how gaps can feel environmentally. I remember seeing the way my brothers and other guys my age would get excited about the very mention of going outside to play football or baseball. That just wasn't me. I wanted conversation and jokes as opposed to roughhouse and competition. But as we each grew through our adolescence, I began noticing this distance between my peers and me growing with us. Real differences between people can often feel like an untraversable canyon.

But why do we care about that distance? I can point it out, show you where it exists, but if we don't understand the connection between that distance and what it creates in our lives then we miss out on integral information.

Public places are a stage for the unaware and straight-up theater for the observer. Mind you, depending on the day, I might be onstage or in the audience. I remember ice-skating once with my friends around Christmastime and I was really picking up some speed coming around the corner. Was I also chanting "Apolo Ohno" à la Schmidt in *New Girl*? It's possible. But you see, what happened was this: I was flying through the crowd of slower skaters, thinking I was really delivering a top-notch bit. I even added some Chris Farley flailing arms to add some over-the-top physical comedy. However, what I wasn't doing was paying attention to the little children as they teetered onto my flight path. I tried to make a last-minute adjustment and ended up face down, sliding on the ice while a chorus of laughs surrounded me. I didn't blame them. In fact, I was only mad I didn't get to see my own fall. Don't worry, nary a child was wounded in my epic splatter—just a little bit of my pride. My attempt at making one group laugh superseded my spatial awareness of another group, and the result was a gnarly fall and a great laugh. Instead of making the joke, I became the joke. Fine line. I traded my unawareness for an achy laugh.

Unawareness can be funny when it comes with a low-grade cost or when it's merely something you're seeing happen *over there*. When it doesn't involve me? Unawareness can be hilarious. Someone walking while texting and tripping over an unseen step. That's funny. And I can say that because I've been that person countless times; to be fair, even a couple times this month. I have tripped frequently throughout my life because I'm either going too fast and have to turn around to speak to whomever I'm with or I'm in my phone vortex and just on autopilot. But if these same unaware actions caused me to walk into traffic or an open manhole, or to hurt another person accidentally—less funny.

As we begin to focus on the distances between people and overall connectedness, we can begin to act accordingly, and with intention. We can close the gap between ourselves and those around us, but the methods with which we do so are entirely up to us and our environment. However, the following *gap-minders* can be great additions to your tool kit.

PUTTING IT INTO PRACTICE: Gap-Minders

- Be the missing link somewhere. If you see someone looking for the restroom at a place you frequent, simply point it out. If you're a New Yorker and see someone looking a little confused while buying their first MetroCard, take a second to walk them through it. See someone trying to join your friend group at a function but there's not a seat? Grab one.
- If your coworker is behind, struggling with a task, or overwhelmed with a project, find one way you can alleviate an element or factor. It could be as simple as helping edit copy, sharing a template you've used in similar projects, or offering a problem-solving ear or just an ear in general. Be helpful in moving someone else toward their finish line.
- The next time you're in a group, choose to engage with and ask questions of someone who feels "most different" from you. Find common ground and notice how it affects your viewpoint of them. It can be as simple as, "Wait, we *both* don't like *Frasier*? Finally, someone who gets it!" Or you might find deeper water: "I didn't realize you basically raised your siblings. I did, too, and I'm just unpacking how it's affected me. How are you holding up?"
- Notice one thing you can do at your job/workplace to take an extra step of care. If you work in retail, it may

be tidying up an area you're not normally responsible for or helping restock when you're normally at the register. If you're already feeling maxed out, don't reach for more. The point is to see a value you can add in your current role without compromising what you already do.

We're moving from merely existing and surviving to participating in and imparting real benefits to the rooms and relationships we're in. To do so from a truly helpful place, we must begin to add a level of empathy to how we see others—that same empathy we need from others in return.

3

If You Only Knew

LIFE IS NO JOKE. Of course, life itself has jokes and loves to tell them. But let's be real, life is not the easiest, and living it can bring a lot of baggage to your doorstep. The rub is in what we do with that accumulated baggage. Life is a collection of experiences with others, and those experiences help inform what we believe about ourselves and the world around us. These beliefs, in turn, sprout behaviors that reflect the belief internalized. So when we encounter someone, we're not only meeting the person but also meeting a collection of their experiences and what those have developed *in* them. Life happens to each of us. We're not immune to the mess of existing with others and the gunk that accrues on a heart when trauma enters the picture.

To begin, let's start with you. I know, a bit assertive, but why waste time?

A question: What kind of gunk do *you* have to scrape off your filter to see clearly in your life?

Now, let's define gunk, in this sense, as any bit of buildup between the heart and head that keeps you from being fully present and able to reach out of yourself to another. Gunk is what keeps you in your own head and in your own way. It obscures your vision and can impede you from noticing essential gaps. If you have to speak confidence in yourself to feel "ready for the day" or possibly even a date, insecurity or possibly an incorrect view of yourself might be the gunk you have to scrape off. It might be that you had an incredibly harmful and formative experience when it came to your confidence, possibly at the hands of someone you trusted or loved deeply. We each have our own lens, our goggles of how we see ourselves and the world around us; we need to disinfect and rinse out anything untrue.

But it can be gross to scrape gunk off anything. And, from experience, I can tell you it gives me the same feeling when I realize I have gunk I have to deal with in myself. I've had to tend to my own gunk. Being a writer was never on my radar. In fact, writing has never been a great joy for me, and if there's a lot on my mind it's hard for me to focus on the task. If I'm living in the cloud of my own question marks, I find the act of writing to be difficult, laborious, and frustrating. When I start playing my own *head games*, I lose ground in present reality.

We each have very different and specific head games we're invited to play by ourselves. How we experience life and what it communicates to us about ourselves gives us baggage. Maybe it's an ex who commented and focused on your weight or a coworker who scoffed at a pitch you made in front of your employer. Then, amid all that baggage and those heavy thoughts swirling around vying for our attention, we're asked to live in a communal world. That's wild, isn't it? Life happens in all its messy glory and we, in the middle of navigating what we're working through in ourselves, are then asked to show up for our fellow humans? But here I am, and here you are. You could be doing a million other things, but you're reading this. We both know people matter most. You and I could be eating at our own buffet of bad feelings, but we're not keeping that from meeting each other here. Well done, you.

We encounter mental bait daily that has to be tamed for us to be present in our own lives, and it can start small. The thought might be as seemingly innocuous as *My hair isn't looking great today.*

But *My hair isn't looking great today* can quickly become *I look bad.* Do you see the distance between the first thought and the landing point? It's quite a jump, but we make those jumps often. Especially if we have experiential evidence that gives our negative thoughts teeth.

In between the initial statement of discontent and the final encasement into belief—*I look bad*—I might have remembered a plethora of times where I felt insecure about my looks. I might recall comments from childhood all the way through the present day and in a second make a judgment about those experiences and what they say about me. Once I see that belief "validated" in the mirror or in comments from others or the ways I'm treated, I cosign the belief and accept it as legit. Then that belief I've adopted will affect my interactions with others, possibly as the first thing I see when I look in the mirror, or even a lingering low-grade malaise to the day. I realize hair may seem like a silly analogy, but it's not for a lot of people and the principle stands. Now let's turn up the heat a tad.

How often do you consider what's going on in the lives of those you interact with on a regular basis? I am talking about allowing what you know, learn, or perceive about another to influence how you engage or respond. Our life experiences and interactions offer us new tools to navigate situations if we're able to see them. And right now, we're going to cover a really important one. Think about your mind like a switchboard with knobs, and "empathy" is the switch we are throwing now. Empathy is referenced often but rarely understood.

A Bad Day's Haze

Imagine being someone else, meeting yourself in the middle of one of your worst days. Chances are, you weren't being your most generous, kind self; maybe you even snapped at the other person. I'll tell you right now, unless I'm careful, the first things to come online when I'm having a *day* are impatience and a sharp tone. I can be curt and sometimes downright condescending when I am at my most overwhelmed. Geez, I hate owning up to that, but it's true. But anyway, back to you and your awful day. Any regrets for how you responded to that person who cut you in line without seeing you? Or maybe even a coworker you ignored, pretended not to hear? Did a family member or close friend get an earful because you misplaced your frustration? Did you drive just a tad more aggressively than you would normally because of some bad news? It can be easy to think we're entitled to acting out based on our "gunk." When we can't control the world, at least we can control our foot on the gas pedal, right? I get that and have absolutely dismissed my behavior with a "I'm just having a *day*, okay?" more times than I'd like to admit. But bad day or not, I'm living through it and there are other people here, too. I'm responsible for my actions and how I make others feel. My point is, I don't get to bring context with me into the world. I just bring myself and how I behave.

Walking into a meeting, I don't get to review a CV of all the goings-on in the participants' lives that would help me understand why someone feels entitled to behave the way they do. But I do get the signals they throw. If I'm looking to "catch" these signals, I can start noticing what's not being said. And then I can start asking questions. Whether it's expressly discussed or not, we are constantly taking in information about those around us and allowing that information to build our perception of them.

It can be as simple as "Keisha is consistently adamant about not having cucumbers in her salad. She must not like them." In its basic form, you are taking in your experiences eating with Keisha, noticing a consistency, and allowing it to form a perception: Keisha doesn't like cucumbers. Upon further examination you might find it's not that she doesn't like cucumbers, she's allergic and doesn't want to make it a focal point of any conversation. It's a small scenario speaking to a larger principle.

There are signals, and there are flares. Let's say Brian is a good buddy of yours, but maybe once a month he asks you if you're mad at him out of nowhere. He calls you up, proceeds with some small chit-chat, and then always winds his way to a question that takes the air out of the convo: "Have I done something—?" Regardless of the context, he's definitely seeking some sort of assurance, maybe without even realizing he's doing it. Maybe he's had multiple people walk out of his life without explanation. Maybe he's seen a pattern of people disappearing when he becomes too inconvenient. It speaks to his history and what he's taken as a belief from it about himself. Brian is still your good buddy. He's just got some experiences he brings with him that can be untangled. Understanding the context for his behavior gives you grace and understanding for what he's still fine-tuning in himself.

What have you learned about those in your life? Your presence in the lives of others has given you information and insight you're able to use to engage in and with . . . or not.

The reality is, we all walk around living through a portion of our own history—we are bringing our side of the story, our woundedness, our defensiveness, maybe even our trauma forward. Sometimes we don't even realize the history we carry with us daily.

I don't share this story often, but I'd like to share it with you now because I think it might be helpful for us to find connections and grace for what we might not know or understand in another. In 2016, while on tour with a close friend who is a performing artist, I was in Washington, DC, for a few days. A group of us were having a nice dinner outside, and I needed to quickly run to a convenience store to grab a few things. On tour you take advantage of pockets of time to get what you need, even if it's between the salad and the main. So I grabbed another friend at the table, and we took off down the sidewalk. It was a warm summer night, and we were approaching the corner. Mid-laugh we heard a gunshot from the street we were about to turn down. My heart sank because it sounded very close. Few times in my life have I had an ominous feeling like this, but a moment later we saw a car slowly round the corner. I don't know if they were moving as slowly as they appeared to be or if that's just how time was behaving at the moment, but it was like this car was covered by a dark cloud.

I didn't think we were the only ones on the sidewalk, but when I looked around, I realized we were completely alone. There wasn't even another car traveling down this section of normally busy road. In the middle of a huge city surrounded by millions, not but a quarter of a mile from our friends, we were alone walking the sidewalk of the oncoming lane. We didn't even have time to try to run or turn around. As the car approached us, it slowed down even more. I saw a man in the back seat leaning forward with what I believe was an AR-15 rifle hanging out a rolled-down window, pointing it in our direction. And if you're squinting, thinking, *Really?* Yes, really. Now here's where it gets interesting.

As this car passed and we made eye contact with the two men in the backseat, the one holding the gun fired two shots from about ten feet away. If I didn't have a witness, I'm not sure I would've believed it either, but both of us heard the shots and felt the air from the barrel of the rifle. They drove off, and my friend and I promptly made it around the corner to safety without saying a word. Once our heart rates slowed enough for us to speak to each other, we went over the events and were incredibly confused by what happened. In retrospect, and after speaking to the police and filing a report, we were told they had been driving around the city shooting blanks at people strictly to terrorize. Well, it worked. Now, if you're ever walking with me and you feel like I'm looking around like a paranoid person, you can understand.

I didn't realize until about a year ago while walking through a parking garage how affected I still was. While walking, I heard a car slowly approaching from behind. Were they probably just looking for a spot to park? Without a doubt. But that old memory came up in my body and before my head or heart could register it, I immediately bolted from in front of that car and into a side door—I mean, I moved *quickly*, like I was living out some *Looney Tunes* scene in real life.

It took me a moment to even recognize what I had done and why. I remember being inside a stairwell of the parking garage immediately after and slowing my breath as I leaned up against the wall between the door and the stairs. As my heart rate lowered, my awareness of my own actions heightened. I almost immediately recognized that through line. I could see that past event and draw a straight line to the reality I was living in. The tendrils of a single day years ago reached into my present and affected me in another city, in another environment. And here's the thing: I'm sure that person behind me had no way to process my bobbing and weaving. In fact, I get a good chuckle when I imagine what could have been going through their head. Most days we leave our bed, house, and comfortable places to go into a world filled with others. We don't get to hand out a list of experiences titled, "Why I Am the Way I Am," and thank goodness. Although I do sometimes imagine taking that proverbial book, one I imagine to be the size of a phone book for most, and throwing it directly at whoever is being unkind or impatient at the moment. Let's just give each other some grace. We all sure do need it.

I don't need to know exactly why your life has been difficult to know that you, a human, have had to face your share of hurt, difficulty, and, yes, trauma. I realize "trauma" can be a word we roll our eyes at if we don't think its meaning is actually represented in the person using it. But I want you to understand that trauma is not defined by your perception of severity or value. It's not defined by my own, either, but by *an experience* that takes place. This experience, producing psychological pain or injury, is contextualized by the life of the one living it and so gains its value. My concern is not in arguing the merit of trauma, or a specific trauma, but merely to say that it exists. It exists in the person you're trying to have patience with, and it exists in you.

To see what I mean, I'd like to call attention to something called a *sequela*. A sequela is an issue, infection, or disease resulting from something previous. So physiologically, let's say you broke your ankle and, because of this breakage, you now favor one side of your body with every step, resulting in real back issues because of the unevenness of your balance, which was first caused by the broken ankle. In this case, you're left with a sequela—back problems—from your broken ankle. This occurs psychologically, too.

A *psychological sequela* is a mental condition brought on as a result of some sort of trauma—it could be a disease, event, injury, or something else that lodges deeply within you. Let's say you witnessed your parents' messy divorce, ending with one of them walking out of your life. This might have left you with a sequela that makes trusting someone and feeling truly safe with a romantic partner difficult. After all, you've seen how messy a breakup can be, you've seen that people can walk away, and you have adopted the belief that avoiding a relationship altogether would save you from that inevitable heartbreak. If this is your story or even a version of it, I'm so sorry. It isn't right that you had to witness and or deal with that, and it's not okay.

Traumatic experiences, with or without our knowing it, can reach into the way we live life now. There are dangerous places I could have let my own trauma lead me. However, I'm a direct by-product of countless others' investment in my life. I'm not too proud to say that I want a healthy relational community. I've lived long enough to say it's absolutely crucial. Crucial to surviving physically? Debatable. Crucial to thriving holistically for the long run? Yes.

When I speak to someone, I'm speaking to a whole life. I'm speaking to an eleven-year-old who may have had his or her heart broken by a parent who left, to a person who left everything to move to a new country and begin a new life, or to someone who never felt believed in and fights to believe in themself to this day. The unavoidable truth is that we don't get to divorce a person's history from our experience with them. Knowing a person's story, or simply choosing to believe they have one worth honoring, will genuinely change the way you engage with the world around you.

Your closest people may not have the ability to communicate the complexities of what they deal with daily. Your coworkers may not tell you about the abusive environments they've trudged through before coming to yours, but knowing each people-filled place is contextualized by individual history gives us an ability to collectively engage from an authentic place. Start listening, start observing. But, be warned, it's harder to snap at someone whose past you've genuinely considered.

It's easier to build a bridge to someone you don't understand or find difficult when you simply choose to add a layer of empathy before casting a judgment or categorizing them. This building of bridges is a foundational principle in succeeding across relational boards, but especially with those you find difficult to work or spend time with. Now, let's make this intimate so we can see this principle close up.

Weigh the Weight

If you're married or in a committed relationship you might already understand this, but let's highlight how you function with another person in a partnership. Each relationship in our life has different access points that allow for varying levels of intimacy. This is why you may speak weekly with whoever delivers your mail, but the conversation limits itself to a few minutes and more surface subjects than you'd discuss with your oldest friend. But that's also why you can't lie to that one coworker you've worked closely with for six years. You could be teeming with sarcasm when you tell your boss you love the new monthly report formats, and if they are unaware and haven't taken a personal interest to know you, they may take your comment at face value. However, the one who knows you, who's taken the time to chat with you on breaks and work with you on projects, knows the truth. Who has more relational equity with you, the supervisor or the coworker?

Each person in your life doesn't know, care, or invest in you equally, so you don't need to carry the weight of each person's perspective of you. Nor do you need to tell every person you know each detail of your life. That's why you weigh the weight of your relationship and allow that to tell you how to proceed. You have the right to reserve the precious parts of you for those you believe genuinely care for you, for those you've come to know you can trust. This is how we protect our hearts from being trampled on or taken for granted, or at least how we do our best to protect them without robbing ourselves of knowing others and being truly known.

If I've upset one of my closest friends, that's a problem. Whatever I've said or done to cause disconnection, I will bridge the gap I caused to the best of my ability. If I've upset someone I interact with while trying to check out of the grocery store, it carries less weight. It's not because that person doesn't matter; it's just that their opinion doesn't carry the same weight. If I have an unaware moment and possibly take too long, don't see someone behind me, or simply have issues in the self-checkout lane (which is frequent), I don't carry that with me throughout the day. It doesn't mean I abandon my intent to be aware and to lean out wherever I am. Whoever experienced me in passing got a momentary impression, and if I followed them throughout a day, I'm sure I'd have notes on a behavioral choice or two of theirs myself. But I take the opportunity to make it right or apologize wherever I can, and if there isn't an opportunity, I move on. Remember, we get to choose whose voices loom loudest in our lives and what we choose to take in or receive from others. If we're able to be aware of and sensitive to our environments, of course we should be. Every bit of minding the gap still stands. It's just that we're not robots of selflessness, and we are going to have oh so many moments we're less than our best.

Our focus is on our attempt, and when we fall short of the goal in that attempt, we don't beat ourselves up. Our intent already places us in a position to win, long-term.

Respond Versus React

Being able to decide whose kindness, correction, and love we genuinely take to heart is foundational to our human experience. We get to decide whom we trust, what qualities we're drawn to in others, those we want to "allow in," and those we don't trust with close proximity. We make those decisions based on our needs and wants; fair enough. But if we base these decisions on the topsoil of behavior and not the depth of earth in a person, we miss so much. You can't be summarized by a behavior or quirk, nor is it fun for you when you are. Although there's responsibility on both relational parts, I'm talking to you about your side of the coin. Where any amount of discord or disconnection takes place, even in a passing interaction, we have some thoughts that happen quite quickly. The *first* thing we decide, without even knowing it, is whether we're going to respond or react. For our purposes, I'd like to define a "response" as an answer given from the center point of who you are. For instance, someone says to you that a project wasn't completed to satisfaction, and you know that it was done to the best of your ability. Instead of reacting with, "Yes, it is!" because you're frustrated, you might calmly reiterate your understanding of what was asked and show proof of all work to that point. Then regardless of the solution needed, you haven't made an extra obstacle out of an outburst. "Reactions" are from-the-hip responses made without first checking in with empathy, reason, or long-term effects.

Parents have to live in the tension of whether to respond or react daily.

When a four-year-old reacts to bedtime with something like, "You're so mean," or "I hate you," it's easy to react. It would be easy to raise your voice and to list out all you do to provide, or you could even immediately punish them. Or you might quickly remind yourself they're four and that their priorities are different than yours. They are doing the best they can at that moment. Having this realization allows you to engage in that moment by responding, not reacting.

Right on the heels of you deciding to either react or respond, a *second* thing happens: an evaluation of cost. "What is the solution here going to cost me?" In this scenario, because you're a parent trying to consider this with an empathetic lens and your child's long-term success in view, you might respond by physically getting on their level and having a conversation about expressing frustration and how to use different words to communicate that frustration. Or you might be at your day's end, and can only say, "Well, I'm sorry to hear those hurtful words. I love you so much, and it's still bedtime." That might be all the parenting you're able to do at the moment without losing your cool, and if so, wonderful. You responded to a person, not reacted to a behavior.

Reiterating that explanation with a lot of love might wash right over them or it might genuinely be a healthy turning point. Either way, you've kept the integrity of who you are in the exchange. In doing so, you not only lead your child to deeper understanding but also add layers of confidence, reliability, and reassurance in your relationship. We trust those who take time to respond to us instead of reacting. Now, what happens if you find yourself impulsively reacting before you have time to respond? Well, believe it or not, there's a route back to health through some good old-fashioned humility. Simply being quick to acknowledge your own reaction to whomever received the brunt of it, sincerely apologizing, and replacing it with a thoughtful response is the straightest line to the other side of that moment.

We also experience this choice to respond or react in other aspects of our lives, in our daily interactions. If you see someone take a parking spot you were clearly about to pull into, there are a few possible courses of action. Sure, you could yell, flip a finger of choice, and feel like you got it off your chest, although no one looks great behaving like that. I've also never seen a reaction like that and thought, *Now* there's *someone I want to get to know better.*

You might take the more passive, yet equally aggressive route, and make faces without saying anything—that's definitely been me. *Oh, they're going to feel every bit of my "mad."* Then I proceed to make intense eye contact, *so they know.* But you know who's left mad in the end? Me. Another option, although less fun, is that I could just let them take the spot. I could then take a deep breath, find another spot, and move on with my day. Maybe I could even add in a thought of, *They might have been in a hurry for a good reason.* That's always helpful in letting the steam out—just believe the best and let go of what you can. Reminding yourself that you don't know their history, trauma, relational world, or mountain of experiences they have to climb to be present in their own life gives you empathy for the moment and an escape hatch from reactionary behavior.

If you're prone to reaction the way I and so many others are, that extra second or two to breathe in some empathy means the difference between thoughtful response and thoughtless reaction. Empathy can act like a protective net keeping our emotional weapons and responses at bay.

Let's quickly go back to the parking lot and add some relational context.

Now let's imagine that the person pulling into "my spot" without noticing me is actually someone I know and love. It changes everything about that moment. Relationships change the very nature of any conflict. If it's my best friend, I'm immediately not frustrated by the moment; I might be amused. If it's someone I know and am in the middle of a disjointed relational time with, it could make me even more angry and prone to react.

Empathy doesn't excuse or make wrong behavior right. However, it does provide an entry point for more understanding because it doesn't close down or put a period where there should be an ellipsis.

If you're someone who is still looking for a sense of real community and intimate relationships, start engaging that level of empathy where you can. If that means you start with your spouse, roommate, or family member, and begin tapping into some empathy before responding, then that's where to start. Let's use a roommate for this example. Most of us have had them. Let's say yours is leaving those dirty dishes, wrinkled clothes, and half-eaten protein bars around because they're dealing with their own mental mountain. You can deal with the dishes and with the mountain by first checking in with empathy: "Hey, how are you feeling these days? I just wanted to check in; anything you need or I can do to help you right now?"

If there's nothing going on and it's simply a behavior, you can address it. "Well, I just noticed that some daily things weren't getting done and that's not like you, so I'm checking in to make sure you're good and see if you need anything. If everything is all right, is there a way we can just get on the same page about the dishes?"

However, if there's something serious going on, you'll most likely be able to tell by the answer, or nonanswer, given. Then you navigate from there and save yourself an explosion or stuffed-in frustration (spoiler alert: it always leaks out). After all, they might really be struggling with a difficult situation on their own. You've now given them a way to escape the torment of something that might feel very lonely. You've used empathy to say, "You are the priority here, so I want to know first and foremost how *you* are." Then you have the opportunity to resolve, or begin to resolve, the whole issue as opposed to punishing a minor symptom. The resolution might just be that they need to express a certain amount of heaviness they're working through and to not be alone in it. You deal with the person first, and get the dishes thrown in. If you deal with the dishes alone, the behavior might be corrected for a bit, but without knowing why it's happening you'll find yourself at the same frustrating crossroad in the future.

I'm a reactor on my bad days, tried and true. Unattended, my reactions jump out of me quicker than any other part of me—far quicker than kindness, understanding, and the measure of love I'm encouraging us all to walk in. I am not someone writing this with an accreditation of PERFECT RESPONDER here to tell you:

I understand the want, and sometimes feel the temptation, to react in the full emotion of what I'm feeling. However, I never like the wreckage of my reaction as much as the result of my response. When I react, I can be a grenade to my own relational life. When I respond with empathy, I build bridges and roadways to others and, inevitably, the infrastructure to my own relational world. As I do, I see legitimate purpose and value in engaging my selfless muscles and exercising them to reach out, support, and build a life focused on others.

PUTTING IT INTO PRACTICE: *Quality Questions*

As we end our time in this chapter, I'd like to give you some opportunities to deepen your empathy for and understanding of others. So here are some *quality questions* I'd like for you to ask when in a conversation with someone with whom you're trying to connect. The point is to engage in an unknown area with someone else and to lead the conversation in a way that gives them space to communicate their feelings authentically and without fear of judgment. I must warn you, these are to be applied *in* a conversation, not at the start or out of nowhere. Please don't pull out your notes app and start rattling off questions. Take a few out for a test drive with your nearest and dearest and note where your conversations go; does this lead you closer to someone or further away? Now, a quick warning: a lot of people aren't the most comfortable talking about themselves. Sometimes, when I try to lean out of myself in order to get to know someone better, they're not ready for it and they try to jump out of the conversation. That's fine, too. This exercise is about getting *you* comfortable using that empathetic muscle, regardless of the response or lack thereof. Even if you ask these questions to yourself and ponder their possible answers, you will find empathy deepening in you.

- When's a time in your life you felt in the very center of where you were supposed to be and what you were supposed to be doing?
- Who is the kindest person you have known?
- What's the first thing you remember believing about yourself? Do you still believe that and why or why not?
- What's been the most meaningful relationship you've held in your life? What about that dynamic brought so much life to yours?
- What's a question you wish someone would ask you?
- When is the last time you felt especially thought of or considered?

As your well of empathy deepens, so will your ability to see situations from beyond the same seat you've always held. This will bring you to a crossroads where you have to decide how far to reach into another's world, to inconvenience yourself. But for that, I suppose you'd need a really good reason. It's a good thing I have a few.

4

An Other Argument

REAL CHANGE IS HARD TO make when you don't directly see the impact it could have in your life. Reorienting our self-focus to an empathetic awareness of others allows us to see our environments more clearly. Empathy changes how we move through our relational worlds and opens up our capacity to engage with anyone in any environment. This capacity for others is what helps you widen your stance in the world. From this stance you can get a better read on another person and where they're at. You can even take in body language and unspoken communication like you may not have before. Because you're viewing others with empathy, you don't see the furrowed brow on your coworker as a sign that he's mad at you like you once did, but instead that he's intensely in thought about something.

Empathy gives us a new place from which to engage with others, to begin an exchange or moment with a new understanding and grace. Next, we will learn to put this new mindset into practice by trading patterns of reaction for new relational rhythms, now rooted in our empathy.

Others at Work

The past several years, I've helped some wonderful organizations address their relational and structural woes, which can manifest in all kinds of ways in the workplace. Recently I was working with an organization that wanted to promote from within into a newly formed leadership role. My consulting partner and I met with dozens of employees to assess skill sets and leadership potential. What I was keeping a keen eye out for was who was trusted by the team and who had the relational equity to create real unified forward momentum, and we found the perfect fit. Although this person had verified skills and deep trust with this organization that smoothed the path for him to succeed in his role, I quickly noticed the golden trait at work—empathy. His relational skills are what made him really shine.

Here's what that looks like in detail: he excelled in his assigned tasks. He knew the major leaders in his industry and had great relationships with previous coworkers and employers. He had made himself familiar with every vertical workflow that would require leadership. He had worked in the organization long enough to know the culture and be sensitive to its traditions and what could be improved, which created major trust with senior leadership—another big win. Most importantly, he was familiar with the workload, capabilities, obstacles, and priorities for each team member. He made it clear that he saw ways to improve productivity and maximize joy for his entire team. In short, he wasn't singly focused on performance and metrics, although he was adept at those things. He also possessed a deep understanding of his coworkers—of their different priorities, strengths, and challenges. He continues to be a stellar leader and has become a valuable mentor for leaders both internally and externally. I'm not surprised. When you lead with empathy and add a dash of hustle, good things happen.

Empathy serves you; it serves those you love, work with, want to please, have no desire to please, and everyone in between. When we check in with our empathy at work, it's like releasing fresh oxygen in the middle of whatever moment you're in.

Where empathy is put to work, more territory opens up for development. When empathy expands in us, so does our capacity to think comprehensively. We create more space for differences in personality, ability, and contribution in our lives. And in the workplace, this space gives us room to see people outside of the single moment we're in—it allows us to meet them where they are and authentically connect them to our collective purpose.

"Allen might not stop humming along to the music in his headphones, but I know he works a double shift on Tuesdays, and this must be what he has to do to get through it. Honestly, I know he works six days a week. He's got to be exhausted. Let me see if I can grab him lunch."

Does grabbing Allen lunch solve a major issue? No. But he now knows you are a thoughtful coworker, a teammate who comes through. Watch what happens. Your sensing his depletion is an application of empathy; your bringing him lunch to take one thing off his to-do list for the day is minding the gap you see—the gap between Allen and his ability to work his role, as opposed to it working him. Because of your application, your awareness, and your applied action, you reveal yourself to be someone advocating for his best, not just how his best serves you and the company as a whole.

Here's the reality: when you start minding the gap, you will find yourself in rarified places others miss and can't even see because they are too busy looking at themselves. How do I know? That's my life. That's my story. That's what I've found to be true. And that can be your story, too.

Exponential Efforts

It's easy to talk about empathy being important in intimate romantic relationships; we can stomach that fairly easily. It's also not too far outside our comfort zone to engage empathetically with those we call friends, family, and even neighbors. When someone you love is overwhelmed, it's easy to find the motivation to genuinely help.

But if I said you can't escape the need for empathy *anywhere*, even in your career, that might be a bit more difficult to digest. When it comes to bringing our emotional intelligence to the workplace, we're mostly encouraged to forgo our emotional responsibilities to those around us in exchange for meeting needs of productivity and efficiency. "Don't worry about everyone else. Get your job done." But what if a shift in awareness and sensitivity to others actually exponentially magnifies and supports your success at work?

Proficiency in an isolated skill set itself doesn't require much empathy on its own. Take, for instance, being an especially skilled athlete. You don't have to care about another person to score a three-pointer on the court. However, for you to play on a team you'll have to learn how to pass the ball. Moving past merely performing a role to working with others in conjunction, even possibly leading others, requires an understanding of and empathy for others' roles. Activating that understanding and empathy as a leader will only help bolster streamlined communication, productivity, and momentum. I don't need to care about the feelings of the wood I'm carving if I build furniture by hand, that's true. However, if I'm building furniture to sell, I have customers and their needs to take into account. What kind of time frame makes sense for me to deliver this dining table? Is the grain of wood I'm thinking about going to splinter after a few years? What's the quality I would want for the price paid and what's expected? Can I actually do what's being asked of me and do it well? These are questions that may involve me and the work I do, yes, but the lens with which I'm answering them is with another in mind first.

Now let's say I decide to grow my furniture-building business and hire a few artisans. The standard I've set will be the starting place for others—culture goes from the top down. So if I haven't established genuine care for my customers, how I do business with them, and the quality of what I produce, why would anyone I hire care? Imagine me telling you to deliver on a quality you don't see me producing. That's some "Do as I say, not as I do" kind of stuff. I'd ring untrue as a leader, which makes perfect kindling for any organizational fire down the road. However, if I build an empathetic team that leans into knowing, intuiting, and stewarding our clients, we set a healthy focus that underpins our dealings as a company. As a result, team members are able to work in a well-functioning, healthy environment based on mutual respect. Clients, too, feel the health in which they are being cared for and in turn develop affinity and goodwill toward the company as a whole. This creates the kind of cycle we want. Health in one area of the organization jump-starts and spurs on the next. This other-focused culture is then reiterated by me knowing, intuiting, and stewarding my employees. I take the same lens that allowed me to think of my clients' needs and expand on this by considering my employees. When the way we do business and the way we treat people are aligned in the health of being "other-focused," we have a clear path to great things.

Now let's take a look at this principle in action. First, I'll showcase a hypothetical issue that might come up for me as a small-business owner. Then we'll look at two potential responses to this issue, one from a solely "bottom-lined" perspective and one that considers the issue holistically and incorporates empathy.

Issue: Fatima's been an anchor employee, and no one serves our clients like she does. She's been asked to join calls after work hours, based on time changes, several times over the past month, and becomes increasingly annoyed and unpleasant the later it gets.

Unempathetic response: We pay her a lot of money and she gets tons of excellent benefits. She has a generous salary, and this is her job. What's her problem?

Empathetic response: It seems Fatima's workload is taking from her personal time and, although I can't guarantee she never needs to stay late, I know we can alleviate that by making sure it's no more than a couple times a month. In the meantime, I'd like for Jeff to shadow her on calls and eventually help share that load. Let's give it a month and then see how Fatima and the team are feeling about this new arrangement.

Of course, I cannot begin to speak to everything that will come up in your work as a leader or business owner, but I can speak to the principles that best serve us when something *does* come up. If you'll notice in the empathetic response, I'm not immediately rescuing Fatima and saying, "Well, then we'll get someone else; don't worry about it." Because I value her and have a bit of understanding of her life, I am more focused on a long-term solution, not the short-sighted one. I take my understanding of her life, which might just be that I know she has a child she doesn't get to see all day and a partner she loves, and that she just needs more of a work/life balance. This also helps me realize the role is too much for one person, and it's time to hire someone Fatima can train to help carry her load. I would look at the other workflows of my employees and see who had the bandwidth to help. And I know that one Fatima might be worth two less productive employees. So if I can hire someone to expand her bandwidth, I'll most likely cover their expenses and net the company an even greater profit under her leadership.

The idea isn't that you spend all your time thinking about the intricacies of your employees' or coworkers' lives and how to make sure they're "good to go." It's simply that as you encounter issues with those you work with or for, or those who work for you, empathy leads to holistic problem-solving. You're not just thinking about profit or productivity, but about what actually helps support that. Any place you employ empathy and genuine care for others will result in tangible health and relational growth.

It might begin with a budding observation: "Christopher seems a bit quieter today and not quite present. I wonder if something's going on outside of work or if he's overwhelmed with ____ project."

This bud begins to bloom when you take that initial sensitivity or thought you had and pair it with a manageable action: "Christopher seems a bit quieter today. I should check on him and just see how he's doing or if there's something he needs." Christopher may have any number of things going on, or just be mentally out of it today and in his own world. However, pairing your observation of "Christopher is a bit quieter today" with a small action that communicates empathy and curiosity will accomplish a few things at once:

1. You'll remind Christopher that he is not alone on his "off" day. If he's just not focused, an empathetic question of concern might be just the "Hey, remember we're at work" reminder he needs on a Monday.
2. You'll apply your empathy and allow that to inform a level of discernment and awareness that garners trust when communicated.
3. You've invested in the actual welfare of Christopher as a person, which increases the value of your relationship. It's an investment of real equity.

I was fortunate enough to watch a leader I sincerely respect for a number of years. She began at a company as an account manager and did that exceedingly well, meanwhile applying every bit of herself and her relational skills. Her intelligence, capability, and strategic mind were clearly visible after a short meeting or conversation. She began getting asked into more strategic meetings, contributing to the overall health of the workplace culture by way of effecting policy, and rose in the environment as the leader she is. She slowly started being pulled into strategic conversations with the owners of the company, and, after several years in various roles, she was eventually entrusted to build and run a new multimillion-dollar arm of this business.

Although she's since moved on to much bigger and better things, I knew her trajectory was set toward real leadership by the way she leaned in to meet her coworkers tangibly from the start. She didn't mess about and had no qualms gently telling someone they were out of line or wrong, but she did so with reason and lack of emotional kindling. Just as small sticks or shards of dry wood quickly help start a fire, so can our emotions make a conversation or confrontation escalate. She used wisdom and had all the skills of a verbal surgeon. More than once I saw her kindly call out clients, vendors, employees, and outdated thinking with such sensitivity that the correction would happen and be received before the offending party even knew they had just been "sat down." I'll tell you, if you ever hear me start a sentence with a calm and kind, "Let me be very clear . . . ," you should know that what follows is some real and direct conversation. I gleaned that one from her, as I did a lot of traits I respect. However, her willingness to speak truth was always undergirded by the relational equity she developed in her workplace and life. Even before she was leading according to the org chart, she knew and made it a point to connect with each employee as she was able. She led because she walked and worked with an intentionality that garnered the respect of a leader; it's who she decided to be. She would stop by an office to check on sick family members; she would go to the desk of the overwhelmed and lend truly helpful guidance. She'd look over emails being written, take a glance at artwork being developed, and legitimately help others, as her knowledge is expansive. She would even remember favorite treats and pop by a desk to drop something special off, just because. She had made her presence invaluable to the work culture, beyond her already excellent capabilities. Her relational skills exponentially sped up her upward movement.

Her promotion wasn't a surprise, and there was an overwhelming sense that her promotion was the company's promotion into another level of health and safety. Employees felt encouraged by her advancement, and several quickly offered up their willingness to work directly for her. She was trustworthy, which meant people could follow her. More than that, she led others from a real place of selflessness. She didn't tell you to do something that wasn't in your best interest or the company's best interest, and that she wasn't willing to do herself. She handled her business with kindness and excellence, and, though she hadn't been making relationships to get ahead, the relational equity she'd built at her workplace helped clear her way to concrete successes: a promotion with a paycheck to match and the respect of her colleagues along the way.

I understand that promotion in the workplace involves so much more than being kind and aware of your coworkers, just like a successful romantic relationship between two people requires much more than being able to enjoy the same movie or laugh at the same joke. For example, a successful relationship requires the ability to have difficult conversations from time to time. Being able to talk to your loved one about why the rent isn't getting paid, without frustration and with genuine kindness, doesn't itself solve the problem of the rent being paid.

But with some kindness and direct conversation, you'll be much more likely to solve the "rent problem" a lot faster as a team, thus closing the gap between two people rather than creating an even larger one (remember that concept from chapter two?). Of course, there may be a number of factors making the issue difficult, but facing them as isolated individuals, instead of as a partnership, won't be one of them.

The reality is that too often I encounter people at later points in their lives who have never sat at the desk above. What's worse is that they have no idea what their lack of "lean in," curiosity, and empathy toward those around them (and their box of stuff) has cost them. When you are your sole focus, you may have a chance to be financially successful and have the material things you want. However, I've spent time with plenty of people who have climbed to the highest points of their financial mountain only to find their relational standing in their own family or group of friends to be as reliable as tropical weather. And this temperamental weather leads to discontentment. Instead of a source of strength, these communities often become a source of stress or pain.

Negating important relational components of your life in exchange for prioritizing your own success is like spending a decade only working out the top part of your body. It doesn't quite make sense—to live or look at. Or better yet, it's like building a beautiful mansion only to fill it with frustrating friendships, relationships that don't go beyond lip-service, and a constant desire for "more." As a result, friendships don't fill your life with joy and camaraderie; they instead drain you.

Now, to see the emptiness of vocational and financial prowess at the expense of others and healthy relationships, let's travel to the Palace of Versailles just before the French Revolution . . . Is everybody okay from that whiplash? I promise this relates.

I love history, especially European history where monarchs are concerned, and aren't they always. I'm fascinated by it all: the Middle Ages, the Renaissance, the Reformation, and the Enlightenment to follow were some wild times, my friends.

One thing I always found incredibly ironic was the court of Versailles during the early 1700s as Europe was in the middle of its Enlightenment era. Do yourself a quick favor and just remind yourself what Versailles looks like; ask Google if you need a refresher. Now that we have that image freshly in our minds—the grandiose architecture, the ornate and incredibly lavish high fashions of the day parading through the halls, the powdered wigs and white lead-painted faces, the intriguing and hushed conversation among courtiers, the grand staircases and ballrooms playing host to an endless parade of entrances and exits—basking in the beauty of it all, can we talk about waste disposal? Because there wasn't much of that going on. I'm talking actual human waste, people, and nowhere to put it. Opulent filth is a phrase that comes to mind.

Now, this phenomenon was not exclusive to Versailles; the most beautiful palaces you can think of in history were once filled with people of high status, adorned with jewels, the latest fashions, and, of course, buckets of perfume to try to mask the smell of excrement and urine, not to mention the never-been-washed clothes. Oh yes, it looked beautiful, and lavish it was, but can you just imagine the funk pervading the air? The dichotomy of the most opulent palace in all of Europe smelling like literal garbage is something that always causes me to wince and shake my head. And it reminds me of how deeply unsatisfying it would be, how superficial, to have all measures of external success but no healthy relationships to support it.

I realize there is a great difference between palaces and the ways we prioritize healthy relational practices. I'm simply saying you might be able to build a beautiful life for yourself. But once you add people to the mix, mingling in the ballroom of where you live out your relationships with friends, in your work environment, and with your family, what's it really like? Is there a stench of what's not been dealt with? Does the atmosphere feel unhealthy, unsavory even? Or is the atmosphere inside of your relational world one that matches what you're trying to build on the outside? This is the risk you run when you prioritize external validation and measures of success over empathy and authentic connection. Using these skills to cultivate a real community is an investment, and one that you may not realize you're lacking until you need it.

You can't always walk yourself out of what life throws your way. You need people to link arms with, even in silence. I'm not talking about offloading the responsibility of your healing to your community. We imbibe the health, or lack thereof, of those with whom we spend our time—one of the many reasons our community matters. Of course, we don't absorb this by osmosis. We absorb by watching, gleaning, noticing, engaging with, and understanding the health and corresponding healthy action or thought of others.

We all need people in our lives to whom we go when we need a bit of love, a break, or encouragement. They're also the ones we go to for advice, support, guidance, and practical help. They're the ones who join us in our endeavors and contribute thoughtfully. What you build in a relational equity portfolio you will end up going to often. That's why I've chosen to argue for your selfless living by letting you see how it directly impacts you. You don't want the cyanide of selfishness in your relational well, I assure you. You'll end up drinking from it.

If you're having a moment of acknowledgment, seeing for the first time the lack of reserve or the unhealthiness of your relational landscape, know that you can change that. Starting now, in fact.

How? As much as you are able to consider another before yourself, that is the degree at which I'm asking you to engage right now. I'm not asking you to drop down and do one hundred empathy push-ups out of nowhere; I'm asking you to start with what you're able to do. If the most empathetic you can be in a day is to simply ask how someone is doing and to listen to their answer, then that's where you're meant to start. You're just not meant to stop there, okay? When you're able to overlay action onto empathy, it changes your relational world. It changes the flow of water; it changes the flow of how you function.

Recently, I saw some budding empathy from a distance and witnessed its effect in real time. I was spending some time in New York City and starting my day by grabbing a coffee, as one does. I'd been into this shop every day for about a week and had enjoyed watching the close-knit community the baristas had established. However, one day as I walked in the manager was getting a bit of an earful from an employee about her coworker. I could tell the manager and employee were close work friends, and the coworker was pulling no punches in her description of this employee's inefficient work practice and some social oddities, saying, in general, they "needed to go." I know each workplace has its intricacies, but I immediately felt bad for the employee they were talking about. However, that was momentary. The manager allowed her coworker to finish, took a beat, and then asked her if she remembered a thoughtful gift this employee had given the coworker during a rough life moment of hers recently. The silence from the coworker was immediate. She quickly softened and said, "That really was quite thoughtful of him. He's not that bad, it's just that when he does _____ I get so frustrated with him." She walked her argument back, leaned out of herself and her own emotions, and traded her vitriol for a desire to help him be genuinely better at his job. The empathy employed weeks previously by the gift-giver made a way for their coworker to navigate some working issues, without even needing to be involved in the conversation. Simultaneously, the manager showed leadership as a balance-provider and careful thinker. Remember, that builds trust. It was like a quiet hush of humility fell over the shop after their exchange. I could tell that processing was in full swing and that a seed had been planted by one thoughtful action. We have patience for those who genuinely care, and that's bankable.

Posture, Physicality, and What It Tells Us

In the previous story about the barista and her colleagues, you'll notice I wasn't directly involved in the situation. I was merely observing. But my observation of a situation, paired with an understanding of body language and tone, allowed me to see far more than two baristas having a conversation. So let's take a closer look at this story with body language in mind, and see what extra insight it can provide about the situation and where the people in it are coming from.

When the conversation started, the barista venting about the coworker was practically flying around the shop. The way she was flinging cups, spilling slightly on her espresso pours, bumping into corners, and showing an overall spatial unawareness of her environment signaled she was in a hectic space mentally. It wasn't crowded in the shop, yet she was still moving like a line was out the door. She waved her hands wildly as she vented and spoke at a decibel level appropriate for a football game. She was unaware of herself, how loud she was speaking, and how she was affecting her space. This told me she was used to working at a stressed pace and probably lived in other parts of her life with the same intensity. Yes, this is a generalization. However, when observing physicality, it does help us to start with what we may recognize and work from there. Although I'm not nailing the entirety of her identity on what I observed, I did allow it to show me a bit of where she was mentally coming from. Her manager, on the other hand, stayed mainly in one place, thoughtfully moving from one station to the next calmly. Her hands were still and measured in their reaching, a stark contrast to her coworker. It was like watching a Pomeranian bounce around a mastiff.

The barista's tone, meanwhile, was rushed, frenetic, and flustered. This showed me she was more or less venting and figuring out how she felt about the situation as she was talking about it. She also rolled her eyes a few times in her sharing—a low-grade arrogant show of judgment. When someone is on an emotional high, either out of joy or frustration, these markers can be present. However, the context of the conversation, the unsteadiness of how she was standing, spoke to an uncertainty in her. It also spoke to the fact that she would be easy to convince otherwise, that she was complaining in unawareness. However, she was quick to concede an "I was wrong about them" when appropriately called on it.

There are a number of reasons the barista could have been keyed up. She may have been overly caffeinated, sure. But it felt different; her physicality, facial expression, and tone all communicated far more about her state of mind than her words did. Bringing the context of my own life along with my observations gave me a shortcut to understanding a situation. I wasn't judging how she was showing up physically in her space, but I was learning from it, and you can do the same. You can understand someone from a distance by observing, "Well, it appears they may be feeling _____ because I can see it in how they're talking or in how they're speaking as if bracing for a harsh response they've gotten before." But when you're the person *in* that sticky conversation, in a moment of difficulty or difference, what's needed? Our good old friend, empathy.

Empathy in Action

As we've discussed, empathy is a muscle. Much like working out your physical body, once your head and heart begin to understand

and practice that empathetic leaning out of yourself and into another person, you'll see how many selfless muscles you have and how strong they are. What's more, you'll begin to see your own strength and stature change. Empathy becomes your new default state (at least most of the time), thanks to each small action you take each day. And before you think, *Well, I don't work out*, let me tell you, I don't enjoy working out either and I never have. However, I make myself because I've learned a few things about "starting to work out" after having gone through periods of forcing myself to do it.

1. My body is literally meant to build muscle that equips me to function better and with real strength in life.
2. I'm a healthier person when I'm working out than when I'm not.
3. Starting is always the worst part.

You'll find a few similar discoveries yourself as you exercise your empathy muscle.

Have you ever tried to have a conversation with someone while they're staring at their phone? They may be physically with you, but as much as they try to multitask and listen to you, you're experiencing their presence through the barrier of something else "more important" to look at than you. You're with them, but you're also kind of not, right? So many of us are used to only engaging halfway, and as a result we're missing out on the experience of being truly present, of connecting. That presence, that being able to be where you are and dialed in with who you're with is an actual decision to exchange *what* feels present to you in your mind to *who* is actually present in front of you.

A person halfway engaged in a conversation misses an awful lot. Have you ever been with a group of friends and seen one trying to tell a story, a joke, or communicate a thought to someone only to realize they're not fully listening? Pay attention to this dynamic in the next group you're in and you'll see a number of responses, but the message received by the person trying to be heard is a version of the same: "X person isn't really listening and what I'm saying isn't important enough for them to hear right now." They may lash out with, "Hey, I'm talking to you." They may calmly stop talking and wait for focus. But the reaction I witness most and the one that breaks a part of my heart is the quiet realization many seem to have: "What I was saying doesn't matter enough." Have you ever seen someone leaning into a conversation and then sitting back in their seat once they realize they're not being heard or regarded? Let's be honest: I've been that person and I'm certain you have, too.

And over time, we allow similar experiences to create a narrative. Remember back to the beginning of this chapter, when we talked about core beliefs forming around our experiences? If I'm seemingly dismissed by my social circles on a regular basis, I can easily begin believing that I myself am worthy of being dismissed. This begins a whole different kind of unravel, but one that is avoidable and unnecessary.

Remember: you're not a victim of unhealthy relationships, loneliness, or isolation. You may have felt that to be true and have every reason on paper to claim it so. But you're here now, and you get to decide what kind of qualities, characteristics, and relationships you want in your life, regardless of what life handed to you.

We've gained an appreciation for empathy, and now we can start building the future. Next, we're going to learn how to leave something behind that's slowing us down.

PUTTING IT INTO PRACTICE: Me-Mitigators

Before we move on to the next chapter, I'd like to give you a few other-minded actions to incorporate into your daily life as often as possible. These are meant to simply disrupt established self-serving rhythms. Some of these *me-mitigators* may seem overly simple, but what I believe you'll find is that they help reorient you to a lifestyle that supports your selfless endeavors and doesn't contradict them.

- Ask more questions than you answer. Want to deepen the relational equity you can draw on with someone, however small it may be? Ask one or two follow-up questions engaged with and tied to the first answer.
- Notice and call attention to a characteristic in someone you respect, just because.
- Decide to "be the last one in" whatever door you walk through.
- Slow your walking pace in public (talking to myself here), drive more cautiously, and physically make room for and be aware of others. You'll also begin noticing how unaware most of the world is—and how easy it actually is to be aware.
- Find one thing to selflessly do for another person each day. Just start with one and don't think about the "bigness" of the action. It can be introducing two friends you think would enjoy each other, writing someone at your work a note encouraging them in their role, or

> simply bringing your friend that candle you know they love from Bath & Body Works . . . just find something.
>
> What you may be surprised to learn is how involved our own motivations can be in each interaction. Taking stock of how we intentionally focus on another will allow us to begin seeing people apart from just how they make us feel, how we feel around them, and whether or not we think their relationship is valuable to us. Now, when we see someone for who they are apart from us, we can ask ourselves: Do we take them in for who they are or try to place them in a category we recognize?

5

Victim Hero People

DO YOU WAKE UP EVERY day and relive the exact same scenarios you experienced yesterday, using the same strategies you employed the day before? Do you engage in the exact same conversations the same way, just pressing "repeat" in your operating system? Of course not.

Now, if you have a toddler or two at home, you may be thinking, *Why yes, yes, I do have the same conversations with them each day*. That's not exactly what I mean, but nonetheless, I feel you. I'm merely trying to highlight an inescapable reality: We don't approach each person or situation the exact same way, we PIVOT when need be . . . and yes, you're welcome for that *Friends* reference.

As we build these empathetic muscles of understanding, as we lean into our worlds and see the options available to us, we will start to see patterns. However, these patterns are not to be confused with categories. You don't call someone the last thing they ate, nor do you define a person by one attribute, moment, mistake, victory, or physical characteristic. We're not one thing. However, that doesn't stop us from categorizing other people, thereby creating relational gaps instead of closing them.

If I'm "the one who gets things done under inconceivable circumstances" and I miss a deadline, then what? If I'm known as the perfectionist and then I mess up on a project, then what? If my identity is built off my performance at work and I'm laid off, then what? Because we don't just categorize others; we confine ourselves to the same restrictions. What does this look like?

Umbrella Identities

When I allow any one attribute, skill, behavior, or character trait to identify me, I must maintain that *one thing* beyond all others. I walk into each room reflecting that one-note identity before anything else and everything I do ends up tucked beneath that. It's one thing to be accomplished at a certain thing, but if that thing becomes an identifying characteristic, the primary lens through which you think of yourself or of someone else, it's easy to fold in the rest of a person underneath that characteristic. Everything falls under the "umbrella" of that one thing, and we (or they) aren't able to see equally valuable parts of ourselves (or others) that don't fit under the "umbrella." Inversely, when we take a person comprehensively for who they are, their collection of characteristics, behaviors, experiences, and overall history, we make room for that person to excel but not be disappointed when they fall short of a specific goal. We recognize their other contributions, character traits, and value them in the context of who they are as a person.

There were a couple years in my early twenties when I felt like most of my conversations with friends included at least a few minutes where I would dole out some sort of combination of solution/advice/strategy. Because of how my life looked at the time, I was giving advice to a wide age range of people. Let's raise our hands if we think I thus assumed I was meant to give advice wherever possible, to whomever possible? Why, yes, I did. I'm a bit red in the face even thinking about it now, truthfully.

It wasn't as if I was walking around with a clipboard of notes I had prepared for people and their situations, but I grew to feel as if my greatest value was being the one who could encourage and give others useful strategies. That's all well and good when the desire to encourage and help resides within my identity, not outside of it, pulling the rest of me along with it. The "umbrella" I had created for myself in giving encouragement or advice began to pull me like an actual umbrella caught in a gust of wind. Because it's one thing to arrive at a conversational place where you can contribute something helpful. It's another to look and search for it, thinking that's the greatest contribution you can offer. My gifting and my vocation had not yet aligned.

We're all leading from somewhere. This idea is commonly used in reference to acting, but I think its application reaches further. Onstage or on-screen, "leading from" refers to the intersection between an actor's motivation and settled physicality, and how that informs their character. A person playing a bodybuilder is going to walk differently than a bookkeeper in most circles. Similarly, a person who is trying to ask you out is going to engage a conversation in a way that communicates their motivation. In this case, that person is leading from a desire to connect more with you. That desire informs their conversation, physicality, eye contact, tone, body language, and more. Consider, for instance, a person you casually encounter in a social interaction who begins to rattle off as many of their accomplishments or accolades as possible. I'm not saying this is a dire offense, but it is like loud gum smacking. Annoying. And in this case, that person's insecurity and longing for validation is the place from which they are operating.

If I were to lead from a crippling need for validation, that would be the undercurrent of my interactions with others. Have I sought validation before? Sure. It's just not my pattern anymore; however, it's a behavior I know and can snap into on a struggling day, without a doubt. It might show up in how I work, leading to my needing each idea to be approved, given a "yes" and high-fived out the door. That need creates an unhealthy environment, because when leaders depend on external validation, they can become stuck in inaction or worse. In relationships, a need for validation might lead to an inability to own mistakes or recognize faults, because being "wrong" is the ultimate fear.

It doesn't matter what I am trying to bring to the table if my umbrella identity takes a seat first. I find this especially important when it comes to those who claim, "I just say it like it is" or, "I'm a truth-teller."

Well, if that's an umbrella identity you hold to in your life, chances are it busts through the door of most relationships you have before you do. In actuality, speaking truth when needed isn't an identity; it's meant to rest within your identity but not walk ahead with the rest of you on a leash. And if I may be a bit candid here, every person who has told me they're a truth-teller likes the truth, sure. But what it seems they like more is being the one to speak it, expose it, or deliver it. Of course, we should speak truth to each other. Speaking the hard truth when needed is a beautiful gift. Speaking hard, curt, or hurtful truth out of context or relationship is reckless.

Whatever your umbrella is—"I'm the reliable one," "I'm funny," "I'm the consistent one," "I'm the smart one"—it can also become a mold you realize you don't always fit. However, because you've prioritized this quality as an identity, your go-to mode will be to try to fulfill that identity in every situation, to try to fit in the mold. When you're unable to "fill the mold" you've believed is yours, you end up in a bit of an identity shuffle.

On a day you can't quite be "the funny one" because you're facing something difficult or you don't feel so "reliable" after missing a project goal, your go-to mode or highlighted quality may shut down altogether when it realizes it can't perform its role. Your identity may start to swing like a pendulum.

"If I'm not this, then am I even _____?"

"But I'm the one who always ____ and now I feel like I've failed because I didn't."

"I can't sustain this all the time. I'm done."

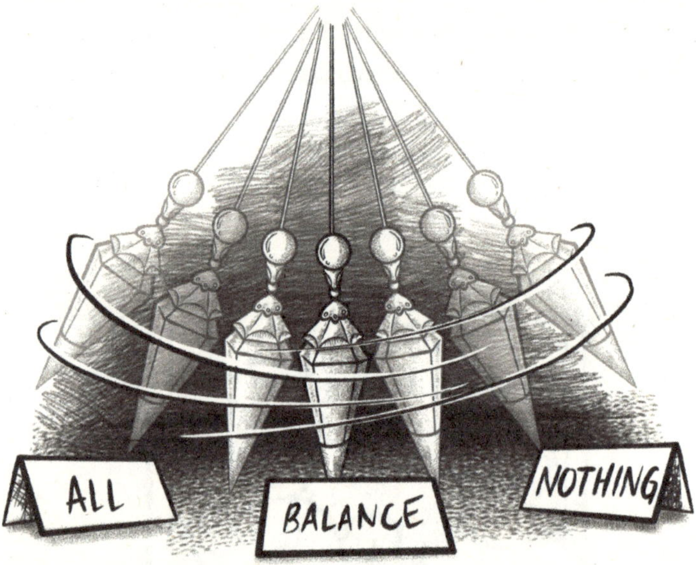

I'm not unfamiliar with this pendulum swing. It's tiring to feel as though one quality, or even a set of them, defines your value and worth to a group, workplace, or family. It's hard to sustain, impossible even. However, when a characteristic sits perfectly in your person, you're able to modulate it for the present need or environment like turning up the volume to an appropriate level. True flexibility. In this way, you're able to decide how, when, and where to let a certain characteristic show itself and shine through in your life and relationships, rather than being confined to its singular nature.

This makes me fondly remember so many people I love from growing up and living in Texas for as long as I did. Hosting parties with kindness and elegance, making food so good it's talked about in perpetuity, hospitality so gracious that the host momentarily blinds themselves to the rudeness of unaware guests—these are highly respected and honored attributes where I'm from. Even this attribute can become a bit of an identifying characteristic, an umbrella identity.

"Oh, that's Mrs. Betsy. Her baby showers are legendary . . . Have you had her caramel cake?"

"You're going to the Badders' home for New Year's Eve? Oh, no one throws a party like them. If she takes the blender out, the best piña colada you've ever had is on its way. Go ahead and cancel your first meeting for the next day."

"We're doing a bake sale for the fire station, and we've got to get Perla's chocolate chip cookies—they're the best."

Of course, the people being referenced would likely appreciate all of these statements as the compliments they're probably intended to be. But if Mrs. Betsy *only* gave herself enough room in life to be the best host, then not fulfilling her "host" role would be at odds with her identity. Instead, Mrs. Betsy embraced the fullness of her gifts. I realize I use a great deal of metaphor in my writing, but Mrs. Betsy is a real person I think of with a fondness so tangible my eyes get a little misty.

Mrs. Betsy was one of the loveliest people I've had the privilege of knowing. I knew her from the time I was born, and I can say with confidence she was an angel alive on Earth.

However, she's no longer with us; I remember when sickness rattled her body. She had to change the ways she did what she loved.

One of her favorite things was to give her famous caramel cakes as Christmas gifts. Our family looked forward to her sweet gift every year. When she became too ill to make cakes, she surprised us by arriving at our home with the handwritten recipe as the gift. She didn't apologize for not being able to do what she once did. Her hosting and generosity of spirit resided in her person. We received the caramel cake and the recipe with the same gratitude. She wasn't Betsy, the host of all hosts. She was Betsy Hall, who happened to enjoy and have a talent for hosting when she was able to do it, but she wasn't prisoner to an umbrella identity of *Host Extraordinaire.* She held her abilities in her hands like tools and used them when needed, but didn't define herself by their usage. She didn't need to be a hosting hero to be herself.

When we landlock ourselves in a characteristic, the internal monologue we have becomes dependent on that attribute being seen and validated, or we in turn feel unseen and invalidated.

Then, if we allow that one attribute to tell us it is most crucial for us in our lives, it will hijack every environment we're in. My modus operandi will always try to usurp what's needed with what's easiest, most familiar, and closest to me. That's why my go-to modes, how I process or react or physically move, have to be balanced and adjusted based on the reality of where I am. I am not some stock character showing up in every scene to be a carbon copy of who I was in the scene or day before.

Notice Nuance

I'm sure you didn't crack this book open to learn about theatrical history, but here you are, nonetheless. A style of storytelling rooted in the sixteenth-century commedia dell'arte of Italy is called pantomime.

These shows normally have a fairly easy plot to follow with minimal guesswork as to the character traits of the cast, because they're all playing quickly recognizable and definable stereotypes for the audience. For instance, the audience immediately recognizes the bad guy because of the snarl on his face and his curled mustache or coattail, the way he sneaks up on his tiptoes, or how he menacingly makes his first entrance. You'll hear loud boos from the audience when he's onstage and cheers when he's vanquished at the end. But everything he does on that stage communicates the essence of his character, "bad guy"—and that's all he needs to be for the story to get told.

I won't bore you with the history of the masks, or the entirety of pantomime, but what is important to note is that stock characters in pantomime will never go against their top-line trait, *their* umbrella identity.

So much of how we tell stories in TV and film and onstage employs stock character rules; we just call them tropes now. Think about a Hallmark Christmas movie, a modern form of pantomime. In about an hour and twenty minutes a complete story needs to unfold. So that means the boss you meet in the first scene doesn't have time to be both stressed about end-of-year numbers and still care about her employees. There isn't time for nuance. For the story's sake it's easier for her to have one character note, for us to know we don't like her, and then move on past the launching pad for our love story.

But friends, the way we absorb stories and categorize characters in a modern fairy tale and how we see and categorize real people can't be the same.

We expect malleability in the workplace and in careers. Let's expect it from ourselves, too. Remember, *PIVOT.*

As we turn on our awareness and begin to see the value of living with others in mind, we're going to feel like a new world's been opened up. As you notice more through a clearer lens, you'll be enlivened by the details you now see and the opportunities that open. You'll begin seeing jewels in everyday life, like the way your dad still blushes when your mom says his name a certain way. You might learn the food preferences and drink orders of the people you see regularly. You may notice your friend actually dislikes a nickname they've been given once you see them with empathetic eyes. You may even learn about your dry cleaner because you take that extra few minutes to speak to her when you sense some sadness in her tone. You might notice how a system at your workplace can be improved after observing similar frustrations with multiple coworkers. You might even see an opportunity at work for a new product, offering, or profit stream that everyone else has missed.

Now let's allow ourselves to veer into some deeper water. Living with this kind of empathetic awareness is like opening up a floodgate of information. With the flood of information and observation, you will be tempted to make quick judgments. This shouldn't come as a surprise, though. Just take a scroll through X (formerly known as Twitter). We're culturally expected to categorize and make judgments on social issues, politics, religion—as if we are experts. Nuance isn't something we hold with much care, and yet, as I hope we've come to understand together, there's nuance to each situation and each person.

Being clued into your environment will allow you to see a much more comprehensive picture of what's going on. You'll begin to collect data and experiences that will inform what you see, leading you to expand what you previously thought to be true with what you're learning to be true through experience. It's not that we "throw it all out." We merely throw out what doesn't serve us, others, and our environments, slowly exchanging what is incomplete or unhealthy with what we've learned is better.

People and People First

Categorizing people only leads to missing out on gems. I'm a bit embarrassed to share this next little bit, because it reveals a major blind spot I've had in my own life. As I've already mentioned, I didn't feel like the most accepted guy growing up in Texas. In many places, football is life and high school football players are celebrities. I was grappling with low self-esteem, uncomfortable in my own skin, and I knew I was a bit different from my peers. Maybe you've felt that way at some point.

In high school, it wasn't just that I wasn't cool or athletic. I felt targeted in a way. There was shame in not fitting in, and I felt marginalized, especially by jocks. It seemed like we had zero common ground. However, in hindsight, a great deal of my confidence and wit came from learning how to verbally spar in school. It created a bit of a pendulum effect in my life. I went from merely defending myself and holding my ground to playing offense.

So I would walk into classrooms I knew to be contentious with not only a comeback or two but with a few sharpened arrows I knew exactly where to shoot. It took me a while to figure out how to wield my newfound power. Isn't that always how it is? When a weakness becomes a strength, it takes a while to learn how to wear it easily. By my senior year I wasn't being bullied anymore and started trading out my wartime tactics to make peace and friends outside of my theatrical bubble. I slowly exchanged the sharpest arrows I had for restraint and empathy. My tools needed to change. They had to. To walk through high school with my verbal fists up was survival. But to walk through life like that, as an adult? Exhausting and isolating.

So what's the point of this story, Cav?

I'm not the same insecure and angry teen I was. I can look at my life and relationships and confidently say I don't function from that place on the daily. Recently, however, I hit a wall I've had up in my life since high school that I didn't even realize was there. I love diversity in friend groups and think it's such a beautiful thing . . . At least, that's what I thought I believed until I began spending time with athletes again in my thirties.

I remember the first time I was introduced by my friend to a professional football player. I was instantly nervous as unexpected remnants of emotion from high school started washing over me. Most people would've been stoked out of their mind, but I was suddenly back in homeroom. I was thinking of every way I could bail and just kept coming up short. I was stuck. And thank goodness for that.

It was like a lasso from my past landed around my neck for a minute. I thought I'd created a life for myself where I could avoid people who mentally took me back to high school. How silly, right? I don't get to choose every single interaction I have, only what I do with them. However, before my mental spin went too far, I quickly reminded myself that I was with a wonderful friend and breathed a little easier. I trusted my friend, so I threw my trigger reaction of "Oh no, football player + me = bad" out in the trash. We all went to dinner, and I quickly felt myself enjoying this guy's company and feeling at ease talking with him.

His personality led with genuine kindness, humility, and quick wit. I relaxed and felt as if I was able to actually connect a bit, and I honestly didn't think much more about it. Over the next year, we hung out in groups several times and I always enjoyed being around him. He just gives off that "loving brother" vibe, and our group quickly welcomed him, his lovely wife, and beautiful family into our world. After that year we were on a trip together and taking a group picture. I was a single person directly surrounded by couples, so I was trying to somewhat give them their space while also finding a place to stand. Oh, my awkwardness was on full display; if you've been *that* single person in a group, I know you know that feeling, too.

As I was trying to not look as uncomfortable as I was, while my face was turning redder by the second, I felt my new friend reach over his wife's shoulders to grab mine and bring me close to them. As he did, he said with sincerity and focus, "Come on, Cav." When I tried to give the, "Oh, I'm fine, I promise" response, he cut me off and pulled me closer. "Come on, we're trying to love you, dammit."

A few things happened at once.

1. I laughed very hard. It was a perfectly loving, appropriate, and funny way to tell me to stop being weird and to scooch in for the picture.
2. His statement legitimately pulled me out of my own head and made me be present where and with whom I was.
3. It flipped on a light switch. I had been withholding friendship and full vulnerability with this person because I had let my past experiences categorize someone before my empathy made space for the entirety of who they really were.

I missed out on seeing him first as a person because I had snapped back into categorizing him by a vocation and culture I don't even know well. At that moment, he met me where I was. May I tell you something? It's not always about me needing to meet others where they are, and that's the twist here. In opening ourselves up to see more than we have before, our responsibility is to lean into others from an empathetic place. But what does it say of my vulnerability if I'm able to extend out to, see, and love another, meanwhile closing down the line of reciprocation, of relationship? If I'm going to be vulnerable enough to leave my own perspective to understand another's, why would I rob someone else of that right?

I needed someone in that moment to pull me out of where I was, because I was being victimized by my own insecurity, feelings of inferiority, longing for partnership, and an overall awareness of physically being alone. I needed a hero. It just so happened the one who came to meet me didn't fit within the preexisting categories I had in my head. That was a reality horse pill to swallow, I assure you. I found myself swinging on yet another pendulum, but now instead of vacillating between "all" or "nothing" when it came to my umbrella identity, I found myself desperately grasping on to the old category that made me comfortable—victimhood.

There I was, fully caught up in my head, in my own selfish "Where do I stand" moment, and someone reached out from where they were to pull me back to reality. It was such a truly kind moment that I didn't have space for it in my experiences. "This guy can't be genuinely this kind to me. He can't actually be my friend who cares that I'm uncomfortable right now. Football players and I don't get on, remember, Cav?" Between you and me, I have spent a lot of time practicing my "lean out" and I'm comfortable being the one to see and meet a social need. In fact, I'm at home when I'm the one surveying a situation and catching ways to help. I'm far less comfortable being seen as needing anything. Pride, am I right? Not the quality I'm most pleased with, but it's definitely one I possess.

But just as I don't allow a specific, mostly positive trait to inform or define the rest of me, I don't let those traits I'm less proud of (pride) define me either. I was incredibly awkward in that moment, downright uncomfortable even, but that moment doesn't define me.

Categorizing is a tool best implemented in the organization of things, not people. In allowing for nuance before judgment, in looking for the whole picture of a person as opposed to what's most quickly seen and recognized, we make room to see the full tapestry of a person.

I do genuinely *mean* tapestry, too. Much like an actual tapestry uses individual threads to create a full picture, so, too, do our experiences form our whole selves.

Each facet of you is like a differently colored and multi-textured thread. How you felt about yourself growing up, the first time you had your heart broken, the important conversations you had with your grandmother, the moment you were twelve and began to see your own ability in sports, the affirmations of people you respect and the wounds caused by them, even the way you respond to people who annoy you—yes, those are threads. What it was like for you growing up; how you were with your peers, family, and authority figures; how they made you feel about yourself—more threads. What you've done to work through your most difficult moments; your skills, attributes, and characteristics—yes, those are threads, too.

Focusing on one thread of stained wool or silk you don't like in your life might make you think the rest of the tapestry follows in line with that disliked thread. However, as you step away from the thread, you see it in context of the whole picture. You're not your worst thread; you are a tapestry with every color and hue pointing to the beautiful and vast nature of you and all you're able to do.

Make Room

We all have people in our lives who are at different points of development within themselves—careers, goals, and the overall picture of who they want to be. However, because we don't usually see the expanse of a person beyond our experiences with them, we can unknowingly put a proverbial ceiling on their potential—if we perceive them as a victim when we first meet, it's easy to limit them in our heads, to always think of them as the victim. For instance, maybe you have a friend who just can't seem to "get it together" in an area of their life. It might be someone trying to settle their career path, someone who has a string of relational blunders, someone who seems to create issues for themselves wherever they go. And let's be real, that might feel like you right now. I know it's felt like me often in life.

That's because we each have different trajectories of growth. We're all "works in progress," and the process of growing into who we're meant to be is just that—a process. We're constantly en route to a newer, more settled and developed, fully fleshed-out version of ourselves. That means on our route we will not always feel like the hero of our own story or someone else's, nor are we merely victims of external circumstances.

We're perfectly positioned to lean out and meet someone exactly where they are, in health, when we understand that we're each people first and foremost. We are not victims, heroes, or one-note, one-dimensional versions of ourselves. In this sense, we each possess the ability to walk in the identity we choose. So yes, we can cast ourselves as a victim and play that role to its end and ours. We can cast ourselves in the hero role and feel the need to carry that weight throughout our lives and fight off the reality that we need others along the way. Instead, why don't we give each other the space and ability to be people first? If we see people first, we don't ignore their entirety by only looking at a portion of who they are. We know how much someone else's limiting view of us can hurt; let's be mindful that we don't create those same confines for another person.

So, if I may, I'd like to just flatly speak to you (this is going to feel direct, and I mean it that way). If we were physically in that little booth I talked about, I'd probably lean in to say, "Hey, can I tell you something because I love you?"

The proudest thing you've ever accomplished doesn't define you. That degree from the Ivy League school, the job and accompanying pay that makes you roll your shoulders back a bit, that ability you have to "save the day" for others, your dependability . . . They don't define you. And every bit of yourself you wish others didn't fully know, the *real* reality of where you struggle to believe better and more for yourself? That doesn't define you either. When we choose to see the entirety of a person, we leave space to meet them wherever they are and not think of any deviation as a betrayal of character. Even more, we make room for who a person *can* be.

PUTTING IT INTO PRACTICE: Category Crushers

As we encourage ourselves to look beyond the surface and restrict our impulse to filter people into categories, we can employ a few tools I'd like to give you now: *category crushers*. These are personal and interpersonal ways to see the breadth of a person, as opposed to merely the most visible parts. Engaging these with every bit of your empathy and understanding will prohibit you from placing someone in a generalized category... stories are too nuanced to fit in one box, and people even more so.

- When encountering a strong personality who is difficult to digest, imagine that person as a young child who had to survive in their environment. Could what you're experiencing in this person be morphed survival tactics, self-preservation, or some lingering trauma? Allow that to give you space for them and notice if it changes your response.
- When leading or working in an environment where perfect performance is validated, be the first to own your mistakes and allow your team to see the mistake through to the solution of that mistake. You'll foster a less limiting environment.
- Look for an opportunity to foster vulnerability with one of the "strongest" people you know by being the first to offer it up in a conversation. Notice how it's

received and what happens. "Dating has been flat-out sad lately. I know there's someone for me, but it feels like I'm doing this all wrong. What was dating like for you before you met ______?" Or even, "There are times when I feel like such an imposter in my job. Have you ever felt that way?" Strong people need to breathe out vulnerability, too, and you may find that providing an open door is exactly what they've needed.

- Do one thing relationally that is outside of your norm. Ask the friend you only go to dinner with to go on a hike with you. Ask the employee who's always looking out for you what you can do for them. If you're a leader, give a young employee an opportunity that would be "out of the norm" for them to get. The idea is to give people different lanes to run in, and to allow that to grow your understanding of them.

Each time you engage your interpersonal skills in a new way, you grow new understanding and expertise in that area. Now, having our empathetic intention set and ourselves free of the need to categorize and simplify people, we can get into the fun of actually reading the room—any room. It all starts with keeping our eyes up.

6

Eyes Up

CAN I LET YOU IN on one of my favorite pastimes? Are you ready to be blown away, shocked, challenged, and equally jealous of the inventive and exciting way I calm my thoughts and heart?

I love to walk.

There, I said it. I know, I know. Epic.

In fact, if I could guarantee myself any block of time in a day, it would be to have at least an hour to walk while processing my thoughts, observing the world around me, and mulling over the most pertinent issues swirling around in my head.

As much as I love time to stroll and think, though, what I love most is the adventure of not knowing who or what I will see as I'm out walking.

I happen to live at the edge of a small lake, so this is where I usually walk. This has afforded me the opportunity to see quite a few wonderful things. Yes, of course, I love saying hello to the three geese that live outside of my building. I've named them Ron,

Sheila, and Corky. (You didn't ask, but now you know.) I also love watching the gentleman with an electric surfboard act like he's flying on the water. I respect his decision, but I mostly respect his balance.

And then there are the rare moments when I encounter people passing me, walking by, or simply sitting on a bench. The ones who grab my attention the most are the ones who look as if life just landed its final right hook to their heart. (Mind you, this is coming from the same guy who only a decade ago could've been regularly seen crying up and down Ninth Avenue in NYC on my way to or from some rough meeting. I know the look because I've seen it reflected in shop windows too many times.)

Recently, I was rounding a corner on one of my walks, deep in thought, and I noticed a woman sitting on a bench, listening to music in speaker mode on her iPhone. She was staring out over the lake with, you know, that look.

I decided to lean out and see what was going on. I tried to approach so she would notice me walking up, but she was so lost in her thoughts, she never looked my way. So I started to drag my feet a little to let her hear me coming. It was my way of saying, "Hey, I'm walking up, and I don't want to scare you."

At that, she registered my presence. To break the ice, I asked, "I don't mean to bother you, but can I ask what song that is you're listening to? I'm into it."

She looked down at her phone and read off the artist's name and the song title. I stood there for a second wondering what to do next. *Nothing like getting to the point*, I thought, so I asked, "What's going on, friend? I can feel you and whatever you're working through feels like a lot."

She burst into tears.

Although I knew it was probably not a conventional next step, I said, "You look like you could use a hug." She nodded. (Sometimes a nod is all we can muster.) She stood, immediately opened her arms, and proceeded to lay her head on my shoulder as she cried into my already sweaty shirt. We stayed like that for a minute.

When she finally composed herself enough to look back up and wipe her eyes, I asked her what was going on.

In the last twenty-four hours, she told me, her husband had been sentenced to federal prison, her sister kicked her out of her house where she had been staying, and she'd received a letter informing her that a storage unit of her things was about to go to auction because she was so far behind on her rent. She'd also found out that she contracted HIV from her husband. She had moved to this sister's house from out of state about four weeks earlier and was trying to get back on her feet, but now she'd received this massive series of blows all at once—it was devastating, as it would have been for anyone.

With each piece of the heartbreak she shared, the more helpless I felt. I wanted to fix everything, and I racked my brain for what I *could* do. But as soon as my mind went running, I realized I was no longer present. I was trying to fix the situation because I was uncomfortable at how overwhelming it was, but that wasn't the task at hand. Presence was.

So I resolved to just be there with her and listen.

After she finished walking me through her landscape of issues and the burden felt a little lighter, she thanked me for taking the time to stop, and we hugged again. We exchanged information, and I told her I'd give her a call after I checked on some resources I might have.

When I got home, I sent her some funds to help cover the next few days, and I also found nonprofit resources she could connect to. She was then working to find long-term housing and her next steps, but she wasn't doing it alone anymore. I wasn't able to fix everything, but I gave her what I could and met her in the middle of a dark day.

I was so glad I made the uncomfortable decision to stop and connect. I feel like it's what being a human being is all about. It's nothing anyone else couldn't have done—it's nothing you couldn't have done had you been there instead of me.

Life can make us feel like we're about to drown every now and then, and we need someone to throw us a lifeline. We underestimate the impact of simply being there for someone else. We need to realize we have an infinite ability to affect someone else's day for the better—but that ability is only as infinite as our willingness. I don't believe humans staunchly say, "No. I'm not helping another person today." I do believe we're often too focused on whatever we are doing or trying to accomplish at the moment to truly see others. Inadvertently, and because of our self-focus, so few of us walk down the street or into a room with our *eyes up*.

Have you ever seen somebody bump into a person or run into something because they were looking down at their phones while they were walking? It's always worth a bit of a laugh, but, truthfully, it's sad, especially if they're walking down the street with another person doing the same thing.

At the same time, it's a pretty simple problem to avoid: just put your phone in your pocket and keep your *eyes up*! But so often, we default to autopilot, which generally means acting on impulse, like the twitch to look at our phones. If we want something better, we have to *choose* something better. Being *eyes up* means being present where you are, physically aware of your surroundings, and astutely focused to meet people and possible needs as they present themselves.

We can decide what we will bring of ourselves by way of attribute, quality, or characteristic into any given situation. We can predetermine how we are going to behave, what we are going to focus on, and with whom we want to spend time. We can decide what makes the most sense for each environment by setting our intentions and staying engaged and present, heeding our hunches along the way.

Imagine yourself going to work, meeting up with friends, or even standing outside the door of a restaurant where you're meeting a date for the first time. Deciding how you want to interact with those you're about to spend time with is no different than choosing an outfit. You can "put on" attitudes and decide how outgoing you are going to be. You can elect to act in a way that will let you be equally confident and fully yourself. You get to choose how present and involved you want to be.

Maybe you are naturally outgoing and live to mingle. Great! I think of my oldest friend here, a person who walks into every room with a level of gregariousness that draws people into his ease. He does this by openly and boldly engaging, sometimes to the point of making me mildly uncomfortable . . . but can I tell you something? It's his secret weapon; I've never seen him fail to get a smile or conversation from someone. In the end, we're laughing, lighter, and my friend has been a part of making it all possible. Maybe you are quieter and have a great feel for the subtext of a conversation. Also great! This makes me think of another dear friend whose ratio of listening to talking is about 3:1. She gives people space to communicate, doesn't get in the way of their expression, and then has a way of saying a poignant and beautiful thing that feels like someone opened a window and allowed the delicious aroma of honeysuckle to waft in.

Wherever you land on the introversion/extroversion spectrum, you have something wonderful to offer any room with someone else in it, so invest your best you! It's about knowing that you bring to people what no one else can bring, and what no one else is meant to. When you make the decision to be *eyes up*, you will increase your influence one interaction at a time. That's why it's the first thing to remember when you walk into any room.

So let's learn exactly how to keep our *eyes up* in practice. It just takes following a few practical principles.

1) Set Your Intention

To make selfless awareness (the foundation of walking through the world *eyes up*) a habit, the first step is to make the decision to practice it. Remember our selfless awareness? Being more aware of others than we are of our own outward agenda or deep-seated wants?

When we focus our awareness outward, our actions begin, as they should, to match what we see. You may think that sounds too simple, but intentional decisions to change our behaviors have a way of changing our lives. But without setting intent, our actions are unanchored, from the hip, and allowed to operate on autopilot.

There are few people I've met who have a natural bent toward being "others-focused," and as far as I'm concerned, these people are just shy of sainthood. For the rest of us—those who don't come by selflessness naturally—deciding to leave selfishness behind requires decisiveness. Setting our intentions and deciding who we are committed to be is the foundation for how we grow. By thinking about how we enter a given situation, we're not playing some part that is fashioned to please others. Instead, we are giving ourselves an opportunity to put our best foot forward by simply deciding to show up as our most caring selves. We're getting out of our own way.

We're all different people with different strengths and weaknesses, different perceptions, and different ways of communicating. Everything I am sharing here should be taken through the lens of who you are and your unique gifts and talents.

For me, let's say I was invited to a high-school friend's wedding. High school wasn't necessarily the best time for me, and going alone to a social event is never my favorite thing. So just as I will be choosy about my appearance, I will be choosy about how I show up. I might say to myself, "Okay, Cav, I know you may be feeling x, y, z—and possibly a, b, c, and d, too—*but* right now there's an opportunity. There are people in this room who are worth your being fully present for, and when you're fully present, you're able to love them well. So *eyes up.*"

Please don't think this is an overnight fix. Getting our eyes off ourselves is not some cheap magic trick to try to distract us from our own problems. I'm not suggesting some form of escapism. Rather, being *eyes up* means being present for someone else while simultaneously giving yourself time to recalibrate and even gain a fresh perspective on your own issues.

Deciding to be *eyes up* gives you permission to take a break from yourself. I'd argue we could all use that sort of break. It does not diminish whatever you are facing in life, but it does allow you to be fully present for someone else and experience the real joy available in that.

But just like in a baseball game, stopping on first base doesn't mean you've scored a run. You have to keep moving through the bases. So now on to second!

2) Pay Attention

I grew up regularly being reminded to "Pay attention!" or "Be aware of your surroundings" before leaving the house. My parents were keen on my siblings and me being safe and equally excited about us being out in the world and not acting like fools bearing their last name. Their concerns were fair. I had a lot of energy as a kid and was quite extroverted. Because I loved to dance around, to sing, to make games wherever I was, I was generally a handful for my more reserved parents.

It wasn't that what I was doing was wrong, just that I would get in the way without realizing it. It's tough for people to get by you when you're flailing your arms around between clothing racks. It wasn't that I was prohibited from playing games, it was just that I needed to be aware while I did it. It wasn't that I couldn't practice the jokes I heard on *Saved by the Bell*, it was just that there was a better time for that than during my brother's backswing at an important golf tournament.

Believe it or not, developing a spatial and practical awareness of others set me up for success, whereas a lack of it usually required me to apologize, backtrack, or make amends in some way. Lack of awareness is costly, and I'm glad my parents patiently steered me toward being more courteous and mindful of others.

I assure you, it becomes easier and easier each time you honestly set your intention to pay attention. The idea is, from time to time, to simply stop and survey where you are. Quickly scan the room and see what you notice. Doing this every so often when in a space with other people is the foundation of learning to read a room. Look at general facial expressions and notice the tone of how people are communicating, the overall atmosphere.

Then on a second scan, begin looking closer. Is someone in the kitchen stuck behind a mound of dishes or frantically working to get a tray of appetizers ready? Is someone in the corner apparently locked into their phone, possibly so they won't have to engage? Is there a child playing alone? Is there an intense conversation going on that is starting to get heated? What is the overall temperature of the room? Is there a tension? Is there an awkwardness you can't place? Are people comfortable? Once you begin asking these questions, you'll begin to see deeper dynamics. In fact, your questions might change as your sight line does: For instance, is that girl with a withdrawn look on her face, physically leaning away from the guy who won't stop talking to her, displaying body language that would suggest she's trying to get out of the conversation?

Simply take stock of what you notice and don't categorize it yet as good, bad, fixable, or anything other than what it is. You're not making any judgments; you're just observing everyone. Think of yourself as a room-reading Padawan—you're just there to notice what you notice. Don't look for patterns; look for individuals. Avoid stereotyping and putting people into boxes or types. Remember, that doesn't serve us well. Simply look and learn, expecting every individual to be unique and offering something no one else can.

Now that you've taken all that in, where can you be most useful and how? Do you still have that gnawing feeling in your gut about that conversation you spotted earlier? There are so many fun and easy ways to break up an uncomfortable conversation. (Obviously, this is circumstantial, but I'll tell you one of my secret weapons in unwiring a tense, volatile, or possibly dangerous scenario is by speaking directly with a calm, low tone and a smile that makes no sense for the intensity of the moment. When you approach a situation with a level head, you can set—or change—the tone.) You may be an expert sous-chef or dishwasher. You may be really great with people and can mitigate awkward conversations or missed connections. You may be incredibly quiet and find it easier to talk with someone else who is shy. Great, find the wallflower nearest you and make them feel at ease. We can't be everything to everyone, but we can share who we are and where we are, and we can do that well. This leads us right into the next step.

3) Ready, Aim, Engage

Now a willingness to be inconvenienced becomes mandatory. Once we've observed and seen the needs in a space, we arrive at a decision point. You're now more aware—what are you going to do about it? There are plenty of people who are perfectly content to observe, notice things, and then do nothing about them. They reach this fork in the road and then simply reroute back to their "me" road.

Don't be that person. Instead take the smaller, unpaved route. (You know, the road less traveled?) It's those who take that more difficult road who end up with deeper relationships, more relational equity, and a growing reputation as a person to trust. But it doesn't come without following up observation with action. It's not always the most fun thing to do, but I assure you, it makes you an MVP wherever you are.

Does your stressed-out coworker need another set of hands and eyes on a project they're overwhelmed by? Ask what they need and offer your help. Is your employer seemingly consumed with a problem? Ask the MVP question: "What can I do to help?" Or better yet, see what needs to be done and do it without being asked. The truth is, if someone appears overloaded or stressed, seeing and acting on a need without asking them to identify it for you first is helpful. Stopping a person clearly navigating a full plate to ask them for direction can be a different sort of additive stress. That's why we should be sensitive enough to our own surroundings and the people in them to know what's needed.

Does someone need help setting the table? Is someone looking for something in the kitchen you can help them find? Is dinner ready and needs to be served? Grab the dishes. Find the hot sauce. Chop the onion. Wipe up the spilled flour or clean up the mess made. Wherever there's a need, there's opportunity to invest in someone else.

The fun begins as you learn more about the people you're consistently around and learn to customize how you help each person. That's the compound-interest effect of social equity, when you contribute not just to your relationship with that person, but to the group of friends as a whole.

This part of living *eyes up*—actively engaging—is what actually invests in your environment. When we take action where we see action needed, we communicate a real buy-in to the people we're with. People just generally feel more comfortable with a helpful and aware person than they do with someone who lives, works, and hangs out in their own world regardless of who's around.

It's at points like this I wish this book could be a two-way conversation. I would love to hear about your individual places and the worlds you inhabit. I know that each place and each group of people have their own needs and their own offerings to the world. It is in that uniqueness the art of building relational equity takes place. It is in the nuances of applying these principles that life is at its fullest.

Which is why it's important to trust your instincts and . . .

4) Heed Your Hunch

As you set your intention to be selfless and use your focus to understand your environment, then pair that with action, you will develop a sensitivity. This sensitivity—often described as intuition—is the connection between what we see with our eyes and what we perceive in our gut. When we heed our hunch, follow our gut, or listen to that quiet inner voice, we take what we sense and translate it into insightful action.

Let's isolate this by looking at it in a few different settings. I think this will help give you an even clearer view of what I mean.

We'll start off in a work setting. If you're in a meeting and a coworker says something awkward that changes the temperature in the room, how can you shift the focus without shaming them or adding to their uneasiness? As you read the room, subtle possibilities will bubble up intuitively. Should you tactfully change the subject? Make a little joke? Ask a thought-provoking question to engage the group in a different direction? Or possibly rephrase what was heard to bring out their real point and give them an opportunity for redemption? All are great options, but which is right for your situation is a matter of guesswork—you have to heed the hunch you formed by reading the room.

Say you're a client rep. How do you take what you've learned about your client and their needs to anticipate what is the next best step for you to benefit them? Maybe you've heard them ask the same question on each call, so you can now offer an answer before asked. Maybe you make notes of the small talk and subjects of interest and ask them questions about their hobbies, their families, or something similar the next time you connect.

If you're in the service industry, how can you observe customers to anticipate needs and wants? Do you have regulars who prefer a certain seating or have a usual order? Do you have a recommendation that you think someone would particularly enjoy based on what you've seen them request before? From the hotel and restaurant industries to anything involving direct customer contact, the difference between good service and fantastic service depends on your ability to intuit what they need and act on it.

One of my dearest friends was a bartender for several years, and I've never seen anyone better at intuiting customer needs and acting accordingly, often to their customers' amazement. I could sit and watch her for hours at a time. It was like watching performance art. While she was taking one order, she would be mixing someone else's drink while noting another patron with an empty glass and intuitively knowing what they wanted. She dropped bills off to those who had let her know they were ready to go from a single glance, asked patrons engaging questions about their lives, gave encouragement to those who were having a rough night, and even kindly cut off those who were overindulging without making them feel embarrassed or ashamed. She stewarded that bar like it was her living room and everyone in it was family. While she had developed many of those skills in service to her job, they were really an extension of her heart. She could have easily "just done her job" and never started acting on her hunches, but she chose something more meaningful and valuable to those around her.

This same principle of "heeding the hunch" applies to our personal relationships as well. People are not carbon copies of each other, and when we choose to know our friends for who they are in reality rather than just in appearance, we become an invaluable ally in their lives. I am very grateful to have friends that span many different walks of life.

Unsurprisingly, I have found that none of them communicate the exact same way. They do not all respond to the same humor; they don't interact the same in social settings; nor do they all need exactly the same thing from me.

If, for example, I have a friend who seems to struggle with insecurity in groups and I sense that struggle, I'll heed the hunch that they may need a little public encouragement. Simply taking a moment to shout out something great about them at the right moment or to tell a story that builds them up in the eyes of others are easy ways I can help. We all know the stories our close friends prefer telling most and a little volley for them to be able to go into it costs nothing. I don't have to announce, "Hey, my buddy here doesn't feel so comfortable in groups so let's all make him feel welcome."

That would bring about the opposite of what I'm looking to achieve. Also, I'd most likely want to keep from making any jokes that might make them look bad or would cause us to be laughing at them instead of with them.

One of my favorite things to do is to set someone up for a compliment. I have to say, it's a lot of fun when it comes off right. The other night, for instance, I was at dinner with a group of friends, and one of them had just started a new relationship that was getting serious. (Usually not something it's easy to openly talk about in a group setting, you know?) Someone made a comment about it, and suddenly all eyes were on her. I knew questions were about to pour in and put her in an awkward, even defensive, place.

We can pretend that's not what it feels like, but sometimes questions feel more like *Meet the Press* than talking with your friends.

I could feel her mounting discomfort, so I turned it into an opportunity to compliment her on how well she had protected the relationship so far and let it develop without outside scrutiny. "I love how you've taken the time to get to know them on your own and safeguarded the beginnings of this relationship." Catching the vibe, people stifled their curiosity and became equally supportive. She calmed, smiled, and then began to volunteer a little about the relationship at her own pace. What could have been an awkward and intrusive moment turned out to be something beautiful.

I have a couple of friends, on the other hand, who, despite hearts of gold, can be painfully direct to the point of it feeling confrontational. More than once have I had to redirect things with someone who didn't know them to keep situations from getting argumentative. I have found a good "Do you mean . . ." or "I hear you saying . . ." sort of question that softens their point enough for the other person to hear it as a suggestion rather than a criticism can go a long way in helping everyone in the conversation meet on the same page. It also just helps lower the blood pressure of a room.

No matter the situation, with my *eyes up*, I can be a part of the solution rather than feed further problems, but that doesn't happen by accident. I have to set my intentions, pay attention, and be ready to engage in the right and most helpful way, and only then can I trust my instincts to tell me what to do next. This willingness to adjust based on what I sense takes me from being a liability to an asset, and when you are valuable to others, those relationships become more valuable to you.

Investing in Others Pays off for Them—and You

Think of living *eyes up* as an investment made with your eyes, ears, heart, and hands. Each time you choose to plug into your empathy and act on what your heart tells you to do, you invest in the health and sustainability of your relationships. Then, as you invest, you simultaneously break selfish defaults, tendencies, and rhythms that keep you from clearly seeing others and keep others from seeing you as significant in their lives.

I like to think of leaning out of ourselves and into the environments around us like cleaning a big window that is between us and the world. Selfishness is the muck that dirties and clouds it, while meeting others with awareness and a selfless willingness to act in their best interest is the cleaning agent that cuts through the grime.

Just remember the four principles of living *eyes up*:

1. Set Your Intention
2. Pay Attention
3. Ready, Aim, Engage
4. Heed Your Hunch

The more you employ this process, the more it will become your default (true north) and a part of how you live.

My challenge to you is to invest in people and to see how that changes your world and level of influence. A rising tide lifts all boats, as the saying goes. Lift up those around you and you are likely to float up to the top with them.

As you do this little by little, you will start to see the haze of selfishness evaporate and what you'll be left with is an invaluable, crystal-clear view of others. Real influence comes from being a clear seer of people. It's the essence of the art of building—and sharing—relational equity.

PUTTING IT INTO PRACTICE:
Easy Engagers

As you now know, there's a difference between existing where you are and being *engaged* where you are. The best way for us to begin shifting our entire selves into living with our *eyes up* is to shift ourselves bit by bit. Start with some *easy engagers* like the following. These are meant to get you moving and participating in your environments, to add value by way of small contribution. We're not trying to turn on some amount of insatiable, "LET ME HELP, I MUST HELP" attitude in ourselves. We're just trying to wear awareness a little more readily and with ease. So back to your *easy engagers*:

- When getting up from a table to refill a beverage, ask the table if anyone needs anything. Do so with a smile and whether or not someone takes you up on it, you will have earned a bit of equity.
- In conversation, if someone begins to speak over you, simply stop talking and allow them to finish, validate and engage with their statement, and then kindly return to your point, story, or thought. If it's been too much time and feels odd going back to your point, simply let it go and try again later. This lowers the stakes for everyone present and makes for an easy environment.

- Begin noticing the preferences of those you meet or work with often: "Lance drinks cold brews and doesn't love tea. Tola isn't much for caffeine, but she does like a mixed nut variety. Our boss likes to sit not at the head of the conference table but just to the right of it." If this learning leads you to action, take the action.
- When in a new and uncomfortable group environment, simply resolve that it's going to be uncomfortable and that's okay. New can be uncomfortable, especially when you're trying on new awareness. So engage where you are in the room/group/office. If you're in line for the buffet, introduce yourself to those walking up with you, allow them to go in front of you, and ask them a question. If you're new to a work environment, make an investment into that atmosphere by simply asking your coworkers what you can do to help the team—outside of your role. If you already see a way to help, don't wait for the invite. If you're at a family function and there's a cousin a bit shyer than the rest, take a few minutes to have a one-on-one conversation and ask about their life beyond the topsoil.

Now that we've started with the "easy," let's get a little more advanced. As you wade into deeper relational waters with empathy and your *eyes up*, you will find a whole new relational playing field. The stakes can be a little higher, but it's on this plane where incredibly effective leaders, negotiators, and relational bridge builders are made.

7

Rules of Engagement

AS I BELIEVE I'VE MENTIONED at every possible opportunity, sports and I have a love/loathe relationship . . . often the latter. But oddly, I do appreciate sports analogies when they make sense in the context of real life. I'd like to try my hand at it. So let's talk about football—a phrase I guarantee you won't hear me say aloud. Let's all savor the moment.

As you know, sports played on a field have clearly marked boundaries. If a receiver, for example, catches a pass and lands out of bounds, the catch doesn't count. Fair play happens within the boundaries. Anything "out of bounds" either doesn't count or hurts your team.

In football, it's illegal for a player to go out of bounds—run along the sideline, then run back in bounds down the field—and be an eligible player to make a play. Instead, players are supposed to get back in bounds as close as possible to where they went out so they can remain part of the game. Otherwise, a player is essentially disqualified until the next play. (I know what you're thinking, and yes, my knowledge of sports is unexpected. Let me remind you, I am from Texas.)

Now let's get out of the stands and onto the field.

Sometimes in life, and in work, people want to be able to cross similar boundary lines and then subsequently become upset when they disqualify themselves. They want to be able to make some advancement by stepping outside the rules of ethics, kindness, honesty, or even simple manners when dealing with other people and advance toward whatever version of a "goal line" they have set for themselves, and then step back in. Starting to follow the rules again mid-play doesn't mean they were never out of bounds. And, often, when someone calls them on it, they get upset. They act as if what they did wasn't out of bounds at all because it got them closer to what they wanted—and they don't seem to care who they hurt or took advantage of in the process.

Or, maybe worse, they don't have anyone in their lives to call them on it.

This is especially sad when they are "breaking the rules" for a good cause or for something that would actually make things better for everyone, but because they have chosen to step out of bounds in terms of some basic relational rules, they have lost their relational equity—their mutually shared relational ground. They have "disqualified" themselves.

Let's take, for example, someone whose job is to cook for a public middle school and also manage the grocery and beverage orders for that school. Let's also imagine that our friend in charge, Martha, is dealing with budget cuts that force her to consider her professional priorities. Martha is passionate about her role and even feels like the students and faculty are hers to care for and nourish. She's been researching different food suppliers and found that a good friend of hers is willing to sell the school a bulk portion of great quality poultry and vegetables, with one catch: they're a new operation and haven't gone through proper channels of getting licensed and approved to distribute said goods. But Martha knows the quality and thus begins ordering directly from her friend, saving the school a great deal of money.

However, a couple months later, the health inspectors come in and ask to see distribution paperwork Martha clearly doesn't have. She explains the scenario and testifies to the quality of her friend's food, as do the children and faculty; however, because Martha skipped part of the process in place and made the decision on her own, she's found herself in a pickle. She sidestepped the protocol for the right reason, but without honoring the process in place; now, Martha's decision has made her a maverick who has jeopardized the safety of the school and its resources, made a legal headache, and overall prolonged the time it would take to resolve the predicament. It may even cost her her job.

Martha found herself in this situation because she tried to resolve a conflict (a good thing) "out of bounds" and on her own (a bad thing). How we approach a conflict or issue—and how we measure the words and actions we use in the midst of it—matters. And as a result of this going out of bounds, Martha wasn't the only one who lost.

In a work environment, this sort of action might get someone fired. In personal relationships, it can lead to a break in friendship, or even a breakup for a couple.

So how do we respond when someone has gone relationally "out of bounds" and a conflict arises? I've seen many of these kinds of situations in my coaching and consulting work, and I've found that setting—and gently but firmly enforcing—our own boundaries is often an effective way to get back on the same page. With that in mind, let me share some of the boundaries I set for myself and the boundaries I encourage others to set. In coaching sessions, we often discuss how to resolve conflicts, especially when they get emotional. Conflict is like that football rule: the more often we're out of bounds, the more we disqualify ourselves from the opportunity to score a "win" for the team. Usually a personal "win" in emotional conflict comes at the expense of someone else. In the end, that doesn't really qualify as an actual win.

Measure Your Words

A dentist who tells you to stop eating sugar "because I'm a dentist and you should listen to me" wouldn't be as effective in their message as one who patiently explains why large amounts of sugar are harmful to your teeth and body. A psychiatrist who is trying to help you curb unhealthy thought patterns wouldn't simply tell you to "Stop it!" or "Just grow up!" Instead, they might ask a series of open-ended questions, hoping to help you recognize the harmfulness of those thought patterns for yourself, and then explore how to change them together with you.

Persuasion is an art and a science. There are certain rules of persuasion that will garner you lasting success—in any endeavor. They are not manipulative, but merely tools you can use to sincerely and clearly communicate. They keep everything in fair play. Let's be real, even the commonplace phrase "Out of line!" points to the truth of this principle. We each have an innate sense of what is "in bounds," relationally, and when someone, or we ourselves, have stepped out of bounds.

As you begin fully investing yourself, you may find yourself smack dab in the middle of a confrontation at work. Let's say a part of your role is finishing a large monthly report, and you wait for each element of this to come in by the last Monday of the month so you can submit the report to your boss on Friday morning. For the past four months, one of your coworkers, Lisa, who's responsible for a large portion of the report's findings, doesn't give you their section until Thursday evening, a full three days late. You've jokingly mentioned how this annoys you; you've asked her kindly to be on time, because, when she doesn't submit her work until the last minute, you have to stay on Thursday night to finish the report. Well, another end-of-month Monday came and went again with no word from Lisa; you followed up with her on Wednesday, but didn't hear back until Thursday night at 7:45 PM when she responded with a flippant, "Here you go." However, you weren't feeling well after work that day and so you went to bed early, waking up to find her email in your inbox. You're not only sick, but now you're late with the report, too.

Before you find yourself knocking on your coworker's desk or door, planning to confront her with this now consistent problem, there are some basic rules and strategies to consider. These will help keep those difficult conversations productive and even keeled, leaving vitriol and emotion in exchange for thoughtfulness, openness, and honesty. In fact, let's start by changing the lingo. Instead of a "confrontation," let's call this conversation a "check-in." Thinking of hard conversations as merely "check-ins" can help it feel like you and your colleague are getting on the same page and joining forces together against a common issue.

I have a few things I remind myself before I go into any uncomfortable meeting or conversation. In my coaching work, these relational reminders serve as conversational boundaries, and when we keep our communication inside of them—when we stay "in bounds"—we'll usually see results we're quite pleased with.

1) Only the Matter Matters

Few things will set you up for success better than deciding exactly what you want to communicate and what's irrelevant to the topic. Think of this as thoughtfully safeguarding the boundaries of a conversation. If you've ever had a hard conversation and found yourself frustrated at its lack of clarity, it's likely because emotions were high and not related to the matter at hand. Don't use a conversation as a Trojan horse to disguise and deliver unrelated, unsettled frustrations, and then release an army of other issues once the other person lets you past their defenses. Instead, set yourself up for success by setting up some—wait for that buzzword again—*boundaries*!

To quickly differentiate between a somewhat universal understanding of boundaries and the boundaries I'm referencing, we have to look at *what* we're putting boundaries around. Personal boundaries such as feelings on personal space, your feelings around those you want in your closest circles, even the ways in which you're able to hear feedback or something difficult—these are indeed boundaries, but not quite what I'm talking about here. The boundaries I want us to look at in this moment are ones we place around *our* behavior, attention, and how we respond to others. For instance, this might mean saying to yourself, *I'm not going to dance around what I mean; I'm going to be direct and kind because that approach is clear and respectful, and an indirect approach feels manipulative.*

Know what you want to address and address it, nothing more. (If you have more issues, save them for another conversation, or at least let the person know how many topics you want to discuss going in and what they are.) Keep discussions about how much it upset you or hurt a friend to a minimum. Solve the problem, not the symptoms. That way your relational table is clear of emotional clutter, and you can look at what's being discussed in a focused, levelheaded way.

When we make these decisions about what is most important before the actual conversation or confrontation, we're able to keep ourselves on task and away from hurtful remarks during the conversation. Emotions are useful, but when they're unchecked or disproportionately invoked in communication, they discredit us and often the point we're attempting to make. (In other words, we've stepped "out of bounds.") Protecting the intent of what you really want to say is necessary to being heard accurately. So let's think. Then think again. Then speak.

In any tricky, serious, or important conversation, know that less is exponentially more. You don't have to say everything you think about a subject, just what's necessary to make a clear point. That's why taking account of what you intend to communicate before you go into a difficult conversation will help streamline your thoughts and keep you on topic. Points of value don't have to be hammered in to be heard. In fact, the more vitriol or passion connected to an idea being discussed, the more the actual point can be lost in the end. Stripping our conversation of anything unhelpful clears a way for both parties to fully understand each other. So think before you speak, and know that being someone valued for their perspective goes hand in hand with being someone who measures their words well, because they know their weight.

2) Absolute Phrases Make You Absolutely Wrong

Being articulate and clear is invaluable. Equally important is avoiding the use of absolute words like "always" or "never" as you engage in a sensitive subject. Absolutes are a divisive part of language that force someone to either agree with what you've said or immediately disagree—and all they need for that is one counterexample. The introduction of absolute phrases is where a lot of conversations go off the rails, because no situation or person is entirely one thing all the time. It feels more like blame than a point for discussion. It's also easy language to disprove and immediately invalidates the integrity of the argument being made.

In an exchange between couples, it's not uncommon to hear one say something like, "You always come home tired and grumpy from your day." Depending who is on the other side, the first thing you might hear in response is something along the lines of, "Always? I *always*, every single night, three hundred and sixty-five days a year, come home grumpy and tired?"

Absolute statements communicate a judgment has already been reached, and when we use them in tense or serious moments, we make the other party feel like they're on trial. No one feels at ease or safe to hear something hard if they simultaneously feel defensive. I'm sure you can think back to a moment or two when you felt as if someone was making a judgment about you that was unfair. I certainly can.

When we feel minimized in a conversation or like we're being characterized by a single flaw or misstep, we don't hear much more than that. If we want an open, healthy dialogue, we have to be responsible for what we're doing to trigger defensive responses, exchanging absolute or sweeping phrases for specific, identifiable examples (a specific behavior and how it makes you feel, what you feel happens relationally when this behavior shows up, and then an openness to be wrong about your perceptions). This will help keep your conversation focused on the issue at hand and thus make it easier to resolve.

3) Examples Are Examples, Not Evidence

As we begin engaging in conversations that highlight a specific concern or find ourselves working through some interpersonal difference, we must lean on data—in relationships, specificity is often illustrated with examples. However, these examples should not be meant to be used as evidence in a trial. They are meant, like an example in a story, to showcase and reinforce a point, with a directly identifiable instance relevant to what's being discussed. Whatever example you give is just one piece of the pie, not the whole thing; nor, in most cases, does one example from one situation portray everything that may be going on.

Say you're working at a nonprofit and you have reason to believe a coworker may be misallocating money; you shouldn't raise your concerns by running into your boss's office yelling, "There's a thief in our midst!" Instead, a more efficient (and tactful) way to address this issue would be to have a few itemized examples of expense reports that don't add up, to inform of particular instances where you've noticed budgetary discrepancies, and then to be open to your boss's interpretation. You might even meet with your supervisor and broach the topic with words like, "I wanted to make you aware of a concern I'm having in regard to some financial reporting discrepancies, so I can know how you'd like me to proceed. There may be something I'm not seeing, but I *am* noticing patterns of spending that concern me. Could you help me make sense of this?"

We're not witnesses called to the stand to give testimony. We're not there to make accusations, just to make sense of a situation that seems "off" in some way. Remember, the issue is the issue, not the person who may be responsible. It's not up to us to discipline, correct, or punish. "Catching people" doing something wrong is not why we first chose to be aware and astute in our environments—it's not what any of this relational work is for. Although there could be repercussions, our goal is never to injure someone else. We're not living *eyes up* so we can be life's detectives and prosecutors. The goal is to add to health, not to dysfunction.

Making sure our argument or point of view is backed by applicable examples, as opposed to using them for emotionally charged accusations, keeps us "in bounds."

What if you need to address cultural dynamics at work? Let's say there's somewhat of a bullying tone from some coworkers and you're addressing it with a manager. You could say something like, "I've noticed two or three times in the last month that Nisha and Bradley were completely shut down in conversation when they felt made fun of or picked on. They've been razzed for their choices in music and movies, for what kind of snacks they like, and for how they pronounce certain words. I wanted to check with you to see if you think there might be value in shifting the way we joke with each other, especially in front of clients? I believe it may help increase our professionalism and save us some awkward moments. What do *you* think?"

You'll notice I didn't make one person the "bad guy." It's not about a personality clash but about a behavior being genuinely hurtful. I'm not using it as an opportunity to bash those who are a part of the problem. I'm simply offering an easy way for an employer to identify actual issues without making villains of anyone in the process. I do this by raising the concern, giving examples of what I mean, and even offering a question to show my mind isn't made up.

But it doesn't end there . . . What if we're wrong about what we've believed to be true?

4) Be Open to Another Interpretation of the Facts

When I say it's important to be open-minded in conflict, I mean it. If you are willing to be wrong as you engage in any precarious conversation, you won't create more problems than you brought to the table to address. Any time you feel a need to communicate something uncomfortable, regardless of the scenario, come into it like you're asking a question. That way no one feels the need to be on guard, and it automatically lowers the emotional temperature of the conversation. The same issue will be covered but with a lot less friction and less likelihood of bumping an emotional hot button by accident.

Sure, you or I could absolutely throw open the door to a buddy's house and say, "Hey! You really acted like a punk Friday night with the crew. You're always talking over people, and you did it to Isabella all night—without even noticing. Did you even see how defeated she was? I did, and you were really out of line. You should apologize!"

Or we could come at it with a much more productive tone: "Hey, can I ask you about last Friday? I've been trying to wrap my head around it and I figured it best to come straight to you. When you started talking about your new neighbor, were you aware that Isabella was in the middle of telling a story? It came across like you were cutting her off a few different times and I know that's not what you meant to do, but it's something I've noticed more than once and wanted to check in with you about it. Something going on with you two, or were you just off? You know I'm here for you. What's going on?"

Sure, your buddy may have been acting like a punk, but giving him the benefit of the doubt sets him up to take responsibility without feeling forced or guilted into it. But there's also a chance there were sides or circumstances we might have missed. The people involved may have already addressed it, your buddy may have just gotten some news that threw him off-kilter, or the two of them may be fine with cutting each other off. Okay, that last one is less likely, but who knows! Cutting each other off to engage in the conversation is a sign of interest and real care in many cultures.

The point is, in most conversations we have, we could be wrong. We could have missed something. We should avoid assumptions. So instead of reaching a verdict all by ourselves, we should act like we're on a fact-finding mission. (As Elizabeth Lesser wisely prompts, "Don't persuade, defend, or interrupt. Be curious, be conversational, be real. And listen." That's pretty solid advice.) No one likes being a vessel for someone's frustrations without an ability to genuinely be a part of addressing their complaints. So any time you're communicating something difficult, leave room for the other person by asking and not telling. Again, avoid absolutes and drawing conclusions from partial evidence. Allow whoever you are speaking with the opportunity to discover the value of what you're saying on their own.

After all, you might be mistaken, and knowing that from the beginning will keep you from paying for it in the end. In this way, we give room for this person to hear how or what they communicated without feeling accused of something that they might not have even realized happened. Then, after being made aware of the issue, give them the opportunity to come back with, "Oh, I didn't notice that at all," or maybe, "You know, I realized as soon as I started talking what I had done. My bad," or even possibly, "I can see why it looks that way, but there's something you're missing."

This approach creates a safe space to have an uncomfortable conversation regardless of the outcome. In a few sentences, we've communicated that we saw something concerning, that we haven't made a judgment about it, and that we're believing the best of the person we're speaking to, even if they weren't at their best in the moment. You make your point, you receive a response, and then you get to decide what to do with it.

Getting the Win-Win

No confrontational encounter should be viewed as a zero-sum game. Be curious . . . and listen. (I know, we already said that, but it bears repeating.) Remember you're not trying to be the winner by making them the loser. You're looking for a healthy solution, a way forward, or better way to operate in general—you're going for the *win-win* (where you both get something you want—or can at least come to a compromise you can both live with).

In business, you don't have to actually like every client. You can have a healthy awareness that they need to make money and you need to make money on the deal. You don't have to make commitments you don't believe in or that aren't in your best interest. But you do need to realize the person you're dealing with is not redeemable, like a coupon, for advancement. That person is a human being. You might not move forward in a business deal, but by focusing on the relational win-win, you will most likely come out of the encounter with a productive working relationship and even the opportunity of future dealings.

Although personal relationships may have different stakes, the approach to finding win-wins is largely similar. Because you're most likely much more motivated to reach a conclusion to your conflict that results in a closer partnership, these same strategies might be easier to reach for. That means making sure you're clear about what you want to say and the actual issue you've noticed or the incongruity you've sensed. It means you're confident enough to say only what you feel you're supposed to without interjecting conclusions, and you're not bogged down in your own bias or emotions. Finally, it means you speak up to people and not down to them, willing to be wrong and giving the benefit of the doubt along the way.

Think about how people shake hands in the United States. I realize this is not some universally accepted "Intent-Behind-the-Handshake," but more times than not in Western culture, a hand presented upward signifies respect and honor, a handshake presented straight on communicates equal footing and mutual respect, and a handshake presented down is somewhat condescending and used to show an amount of dominance.

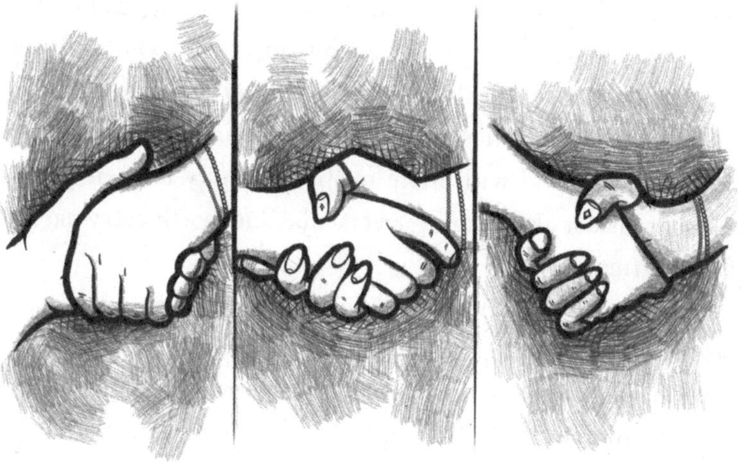

We communicate this honor and dishonor in how we speak as well . . . and with a great deal more variety of nuance than demonstrated with handshakes.

Addressing what you see and having uncomfortable conversations will take some practice, but I promise it's something you're well equipped to do. I know that holding to boundaries while guarding the words leaving your mouth can feel as tedious as driving a cliffside highway in the midst of a storm. But know that you can navigate the road, and soon, if you stay consistent in moving forward as you keep your eyes on the road ahead, the clouds will part. Only then will you be able to see why the view was worth the drive.

In truth, you'll end up in many beautiful relational places other people never get to go because the way seems harrowing and too difficult. Conflict is not a roadblock. It is simply a curve in the road.

What most of us don't know, and what I desperately want you to know, is that on the other side of each difficult moment or hard truth communicated, there's a new relational viewpoint waiting to be discovered that reveals an incredible new landscape: the win-win. Where both parties walk out of a difficult conversation more whole, in sync, and with more relational equity in their pockets. That new vista is always quite spectacular and worth every hardship of the journey.

Intentionality with consistency will begin shaping us into a person suited to sense, pause, and react to others with focus and a level head. These qualities are the same ones that help position us for promotion, increased influence, deeper relationships, and greater relational equity.

This incremental growth and willingness to make small adjustments in ourselves along with the ways we engage with others make us people of great capacity. When we consistently show up ready to learn about others and meet needs in our environments, we are often entrusted with increasing authority. Why is that? Because someone who can be trusted to operate within relational boundaries with people is guaranteed to be trusted with much more.

PUTTING IT INTO PRACTICE: *Dialogue Decompressors*

Now that we've dug into what healthy confrontation looks like, I'd like to leave you with some *dialogue decompressors*—ways to alleviate the tension, intensity, and emotional climate of whatever hard conversation you're having. Think of these as ways to open a window, release the steam in a pressure cooker, or to simply improve the quality of "air" (conversation) being ingested.

- When you hear a statement you'd normally react to from a heightened place, simply take a breath so that your speaking is level. "I heard you say ________, but it felt like you said ________. Is there any way you can say that again? I just want to make sure I'm hearing you wholly and correctly." This ensures you don't respond solely based on what you heard the first time. It also gives the other party a chance to reshape their language or intent.
- When addressing a problematic situation or behavior, assume the person you're talking to about their behavior is hearing it for the first time. Allow that benefit of the doubt to lead your gentleness in the conversation and your belief in them while having the discussion. You'll be surprised how it shapes your conversation and immediately lowers the stakes.
- If a conversation gets too heated, restore the balance and gain trust by not allowing yourself to be escalated. Decide on a measured voice, low and calm. Decide on concise and clear communication, free of "I feel" and absolutes like "You always." You'll find yourself holding great relational equity once the intensity has subsided. Use this as an opportunity to lead and set a behavioral tone in the conversation.

- When you feel "off" in a relationship and you know you've stepped out of line, don't wait until things boil up and over to address it. Quickly own your part and lower the stakes of your mistakes by taking their power away in your relationship. "Hey, I know we haven't talked much in the last week, and I was thinking about the last conversation we had. I was trying to be funny when I said ______, and in hindsight, it was a thoughtless thing to say. Will you forgive me?" That's a powerful thing to do, my friend.
- If you encounter someone in your life who seems less than well intentioned and your gut is burning with that "Oh, this person has bad motives" feeling—use some eye contact; it's one of the best tools we have. While you engage with them, don't lose their eyes; they'll tell you an awful lot. That's because holding direct eye contact is one of the most low-key and effective ways to let someone feel truly seen, good or bad. Ask questions, get empathetic, but always come back to the eyes. You'll learn more about what is *actually* going on in a person when you make eye contact nonnegotiable.

Now that we've begun filling our relational toolboxes with some real strategies for the difficult situations and conversations we all find ourselves in, how do we begin thinking toward a whole life and how we want the world of our relationships to look? Let's get into it.

8

A Styled Life

UP UNTIL NOW, THE FOCUS of this book has been on getting equipped to handle what's thrown at you relationally, wherever people are. How do you thoughtfully respond to gnarly situations at work, how do you lean into a sensitive conversation with a loved one, how do you notice the body language available for your reading, how do you use the information you take in to lead you to thoughtful action? Next, we're going to move beyond our response to environments, scenarios, and the people in them. We've talked about relational equity and how many of the skills we've learned so far will help us build it. Now that we're growing together in our ability to survey a room, to thoughtfully interact with the people in it, you get to decide what you'll do with the influence you gain. So let's move on to why we're here. Let's talk about you.

Jokes aside, every bit of abstract analogy aside, what sort of relational life do you want for yourself? You may not have thought about this before, and if not—wonderful! We've got a clean slate on which to sketch, design, and build.

For the rest of this book, this is our anchoring question, one we're going to look at in a few ways. So first, let's start with the qualities, atmospheres, relational practices, and tendencies we want to have in our lives . . . as well as those we'd rather not. This will require intentionality on our part, because we want to choose the kinds of qualities, environments, and people in our lives that support our pursuits and contribute positively to the quality of our lives, not detract from it.

To illustrate what I mean by adding intentionality to what we want to see in our lives, let's start small. I'm a daily coffee-grabber and most days begin with me running by to snag a latte from my local spot. Well, when a new coffee shop opened right by me, I was ecstatic, because who doesn't want a place where they can walk in and feel known and like part of the "communal family"—steps from home? My ultimate goal was to have a good relationship with the shop and the baristas in it, so I needed to be intentional to see that goal met.

As soon as this new shop opened, I began going regularly and would try to find a question I could ask or one meaningful way to engage each time I visited. I slowly began to know the staff and they began to know me. We'd have a few minutes of a kind and uplifting exchange each day and I began to genuinely look forward to popping in, seeing my barista buds, and being on my way. I truly had forgotten my initial motivation of having "my spot" in town and just enjoyed getting to know this crew of unique people. Then one day I popped in and it was like this place became *the* place to grab coffee overnight. There was a line out the door, and I began waiting. I was on my phone and just heard a "Cav!" come from behind the counter. They started making my drink as soon as they saw me walk up and knew, as I did, that the line was nuts. I didn't ask them to prioritize me or my desperate need for caffeine. But consistently and intentionally showing up with kindness and a willingness to engage created equity I benefited from down the line. Just like we invest in people, we invest in environments. I'm now getting to do this again at a farmers market nearby. I've made it a weekly stop of mine and have been casually getting to know the vendors. Rasheeda makes the most incredible candles, and after striking up a few intentional conversations, she now gives me a new sample to test out every week. Does she know that I also want to help get her candles in stores and sold through a number of shows I'm working on? No, she doesn't, and I didn't either until a few weeks after making the decision to invest in this specific environment I'm in.

Beyond small investments in physical environments—at my coffee shop or with the vendors at my farmers market—I also have the ability to invest in the future of my relational environments, and to design them in a way that's fulfilling to me. You do, too.

Your life and its relational components are not some oversized garments handed down to you from generations past. You're not trapped wearing that ruffled gown from the eighties your mom still has in her closet or that suit your dad said was "about" your size. At this point in your adulthood, whatever that looks like for you right now, you have the ability to decide what you want to prioritize in your relational world. To do this, you can start by looking at the relationships in your life—what's working and what's not.

Here are a few questions I'd like for you to ask yourself and thoughtfully consider:

What's working in my relationships?

Example: I've noticed Adana and I are able to be fully transparent with each other and we don't get mad if one of us forgets to text back. She's hard to offend and I'd like more of that in my life.

Example: I really like how Manuel doesn't talk negatively about people. He doesn't join in on a venting session and that makes me want more friendships I feel safe in.

Example: I love how Fran can talk for an hour, if not longer, about another person, and never need to be asked a question about herself in conversations. She's genuinely interested in others. I'd like to see more of that.

Do I have any relational nonnegotiables?

Example: Passive-aggressive behavior makes me feel manipulated in relationships, so honesty and direct communication are nonnegotiable.

Example: People who can't communicate their frustration without raising their voices or going "too far" make me feel unsafe . . . or just tired.

Example: People who expect one-sided friendships and aren't actively investing in the friendship from their side aren't sustainable for me in the long run.

Do I feel trapped in any relationships?

Example: When I get together with my friends, all we do is gossip and I don't know how to stop it.

Example: It feels like the coworker I've bonded with is becoming controlling about who I become close with in the office. They've started gatekeeping conversations.

What's important to me, relationally?

Example: I feel fullest when I'm around those who are genuinely engaged with others and know how to ask a good question.

Example: I want to surround myself with people who simply do what they say they're going to do. I want people whose word I can rely on.

Once we take stock in what our worlds—relational and otherwise—look like, we can begin to think about what we *want* them to look like in the future. Beyond where we are, where do we want to be?

Let's paint a little picture, shall we? Say you spend a few decades prioritizing your goals, getting the things you want career-wise, but think little about the relationships of your life. The place you "get to" is amazing, yes, but shared with and appreciated by whom? You, yourself, and you? There isn't a goal met or career finish line achieved that isn't made sweeter by community, and isn't inevitably made miserable by isolation. I can enjoy a stunning sunset by myself, which I have and will continue to do. But the ones I remember taking in like a healing tonic or hitting me like a fresh breeze, the ones that reminded me life was going to continue and allowed me to take a breath? Those have been shared with others. It's not the way the clouds broke and the color poured through that I always remember, although that's what I always snap a picture of—it's the way the light bounces off the faces of those I love and how we share it, reflecting that love back to each other.

Our relational investments don't just add to our highs, though—they can help get us through the low points, too. Relationships are like fortresses and when life turns on its head, you quickly realize the sort of fortresses you've built. It might be that the house you built has holes in the roof, and you don't realize it until the first time it rains. (I don't know why I picture you as a homesteader. It could be all of the *Life Below Zero* I watch. But I digress.) If you have a friend you've only ever laughed and shared frivolous or fun times with, it might be difficult for you to think of this person capable of handling heavier matters as they appear in your life. If you're looking for advancement at work but have only ever shown up in your leader's office to complain or ask for time off, it's difficult to then go to that same leader and ask for a promotion—and expect anything less than a question mark–face. However, if there's an established history of you showing up for the team, developing relational equity with that team, prioritizing your role, and then investing elsewhere in the company where you have bandwidth, that's a much different conversation. You're going in to negotiate with money already on the table.

The mess happens when that relational equity hasn't been built, hasn't been established or prioritized, and then some sort of breakdown happens. And spoiler alert, breakdowns *will* happen. As we walked through in chapter three, achieving financial success without prioritizing relationships can translate into a loneliness that genuinely isn't worth it. Like a game of "King of the Hill," the one on top is solely responsible for staying at the top. It leads to a "one against all" mentality. If you are the king of that hill and everyone else, the "all" surrounding you, are not true friends, it's a near guarantee you'll be pulled down.

Establish a pattern of health and you'll find that it makes a way for you through a hard moment. Before we get into the granular nature of what I'm talking about, I'm going to speak to my millennial friends specifically about a Drew Barrymore movie I feel we should all know and love . . . Yes, of course I'm referring to the classic Cinderella remake of the late nineties, *Ever After*.

Toward the end of the film Ms. Barrymore's character, Danielle, has finally married her prince and her stepmother and stepsister are brought in before the king and queen to answer for lying to them, as well as their overall cruel behavior. Danielle's stepmother is a baroness in the film so before stripping them of their titles and sentencing them to a life of servitude, the queen asks if someone in the court would speak up for them, to vouch for their character. After looking around the room to the snarling faces of those the baroness had discounted, those she'd been unaware of and looked past for years, the baroness faintly quips, "Seems to be quite a few people out of town." In the end, the only person able to speak to the stepmother's character is Danielle herself. In her self-consumption, Danielle's stepmother created the very isolation that sealed her fate in the end. The reason phrases like "You reap what you sow" or "Lie in the bed you made" are commonplace is because they speak to a truth we know and accept: you don't get to act however you want and then be surprised when an appropriate outcome finds you.

Now I realize I'm talking about a movie you might not have seen, but we see this scene play out in real life, too. When we have built up and patterned a life focused on ourselves, we are the ones responsible for the great relational dissonance we feel when breakdown comes. I've even seen this scenario play out organizationally. I think of one leader who was internally known for being incredibly disrespectful to vendors and partners for events. This person slowly made enemies for themselves across multiple verticals. When they finally slipped up and showed their hand (they revealed themselves to be engaging in false representation and siphoning of funds), their coworkers essentially threw their hands up and said, "Well, isn't that a shame." Not one person stood up to say, "Now wait a second, we can't lose them." In fact, it felt like people stood just to open the door and watch them walk out. I know that's a far cry from where most of us are in our unawareness, but a vacuum of opinion is a vacuum regardless and that person spent a great deal of time "killing it" on their own . . . until they truly were on their own. They thought only about themselves and were left with only themselves in the end. I often wonder, if that person had known years previously that they could change how they operated with people in their relational world, that they could be known as a healthy and trustworthy individual, would they?

Now Wait a Minute

It's not difficult to find ourselves in ruts of behavior and unhealthy relationships only to look up at some point in life with a puzzled, "Now how exactly did I get *here*?" How did I end up feeling like a stranger in my own family? How did I work for six years in the same role and not grow past it to another? Whatever your "Now wait a minute" moment is, you have the ability to start changing the reality you live in. It doesn't have to stay the same for you going forward. Yes, it'll require some work, but you're not stuck in "how it's been." You, as a growingly empathetic, selflessly aware person, have taken seven chapters to thoughtfully learn how to lean *out* of yourself and *in* to others. Now it's time to get out the relational fabric swatches and think about the selfless behaviors, characteristics, and the overall intent you choose to suit up in—and how you'd like to see them incorporated into your life.

So many people live their lives not seeing the connection between how they actually steward the people around them and the relational world they live in. In other words, they aren't aware that they can support their own holistic personal growth, health, and joy by thoughtfully investing time and intent into stewarding the relationships that align with what they want in life.

I'd like to tell you about a trip I recently went on. I was with a few friends on vacation and our host wanted to introduce us to another friend group that was vacationing in the same area. I was surprised to learn the group we were being introduced to was that of a very well-known entertainer. I'll simply say that I was a fan of this person for a couple decades. Now, putting my fandom aside, I decided to get intentional with how I approached the new group by trying to show up in kindness, normalcy, and authenticity. I'm not sure how normal I am or even what that really means, but I did my best. We arrived where they were staying for dinner and drinks to follow and were immediately made to feel welcome, and I felt a true openness to friendship. Our two friend groups ended up spending a few nights of the vacation hanging out, and there were some real gems I enjoyed getting to know in that crew. But you know what? There were also a few in there I wouldn't trust to watch a pet rock.

I realize that's a strong thing to say, but I do mean it. At this point you're familiar with how I assess a room and what I'm looking for as I keep my *eyes up*. While I look for authentic gems inside of a person, I'm also attempting to sift out the fool's gold and false treasure—dishonesty, arrogance, and entitlement. In *this* very specific atmosphere of influence and celebrity, the genuine and disingenuous often coexist. The genuine aren't just there to gain something, and you can feel it in their presence; you can see and hear it in their person. The disingenuous are there for themselves, whether it be advancement, proximity to perceived power, financial benefits, or to take advantage in a specific way.

Whether intentionally or unintentionally, those who have ulterior motives may perform outwardly as though they don't. They present to the person whose affections they're trying to garner as one way, a kind and thoughtfully engaged listener maybe, and then when in a different environment you see that to be a trait only pulled out for "those of importance." I can often see true character when the celebrity leaves the room. How does someone act when it's "just" the remnants in the room? How are waiters spoken to when the table is being cleared? How is someone when the focus isn't on them? That developed sensitivity to be able to connect someone's words with their body language, eye contact, disposition, tone, and demeanor is crucial in getting a clearer picture of them.

Being aware of these things doesn't mean we're some deputy of justice in a certain area, that *we're the ones meant to correct and make right.* But it's valuable information to have as we're determining what kind of relational world we want to build.

After a few days, it became increasingly clear to me that a couple of people in this entertainer's life had some mixed agendas. Friend groups surrounding any sort of influential person are fraught with interesting dynamics. As we learned in the last chapter, it's possible to have hard conversations to address someone who's gone relationally "out of bounds," and these conversations often end up bringing more health and honesty to everyone nearby.

When they're not addressed, however, the whole culture of that friend group can feel like an overgrown garden with weeds choking out any new life. No, people are not weeds, but yes, they sure can act like them. Yes, I believe there are gems of character to be found in each of us, but there are also people who have chosen themselves above all else. It can be dangerous to let these people into your inner circle.

On the last day of our trip, my friend and I found ourselves in conversation with one such untrustworthy pet-rock-babysitter. This person had spent more than a few hours over the course of several days trying to impress my friends with the money they'd made and the connections they had, all with a haughtiness that made it difficult to stomach, even for a few moments. Our new entertainer friend sat quietly in a chair right behind this person as they performatively told us stories that genuinely made himself and friends look quite shallow, all the while goading us into engagement. It was tiring. You know who I saw this conversation to be equally tiring to? Entertainer friend.

Well, obviously, I took this as an invitation to correct our course. You understand. There is only so much nonsense that can fill the air before someone needs to set boundaries. In this case, me.

After several minutes of listening to this person simultaneously boast about their magnanimous nature with their friends and complain about their lack of loyalty or maturity, I had to shift the vibe in our hang. It felt heavy and unhealthy. My response, although directed to him, was meant as an atmospheric shift for the entire group. When I found a break in his rant, I jumped in with something like, "Well, that *does* sound like a bummer, yes. But I also know we get to choose who we do life with and when we meet people of quality who are genuinely about others more than themselves, that becomes the new floor of what we're relationally willing to accept in our lives." I gestured to my close friend, "The reason we've been friends as long as we have is that we prioritize similar things in friendship and in our relationships, period. We both want people in our lives who are thoughtful of others, quick to forgive and to believe the best, and that's the culture we want our relational worlds to be marked by."

Directly, I was trying to get us out of this black hole of a conversation. It was tangibly wearing the group down; you could see it on the disengaged faces of those sitting with us. Indirectly, I was trying to put some wind in the relational sails of our new friends, to encourage them into a healthier and fuller community by showing it as a real and attainable option. When you've defined relational values for yourself and what you're looking for in others, you recognize and safeguard the relationships that share your values. In short, if you want comprehensively good and healthy friends, first *be* that good friend and understand how you define that. Only then will you be able to find more people who share your values and steer away from those who do not. You can have the sort of life-giving relationships you want. But you have to decide you want it.

You don't have to be wealthy or famous or successful or in a relationship or the best or the skinniest or the most beautiful to have an actual right to give your time, effort, love, energy, care, affection, humor, investments, vulnerability, kindness, and thoughtfulness away to whomever you choose. You do not have to stay in the same relational dynamics you've come to know. You are not trapped. You may feel subject to your environment, upbringing, or some relational dead ends at which you've found yourself, but regardless of how small and confining that relational room might feel, no matter how landlocked you feel by unhealth—you can always move toward health. And when you set that health in motion, you gain influence. As you trust yourself and the tools you've gained, others learn to trust you, too.

At this point, we've seen how the quality of our lives and our relationships stretch far beyond ourselves. Now that we have a fuller picture of the whole relational landscape—including other people, our environments, and the roles we play—we begin to see how much agency we really have. So now that we've walked this far together, now that we've been sitting in that proverbial corner booth together for chapter after chapter, I'd like to simply ask you, friend, what do you want for your life relationally?

For starters, think about what you want the environments you live in to look like in ten years. What are some characteristics and traits you'd like to see in that version of your life—both in the people and in your relationships with them?

By this point, you've probably picked up on some of the traits that would be important to me. Yes, I'm presenting a set of tools I believe to be crucial to your advancement—social, business, and personal. However, I don't come to this conversation unbiased. Not everything I've chosen to be of utmost relational importance to me should bear the same weight in your relational life. You might not need friends who can speak in quotes from *Mrs. Doubtfire* or *Sister Act II* at will. I do.

Although I'm kidding to an extent, I'm not joking about thoughtfully considering what you want to prioritize in your overall relational culture. I began putting the following list together in my early twenties. They're my *cultural priorities*, and although they've changed and grown as I have, there are a few defining wants I'd like to highlight.

- I want a community that genuinely celebrates others' wins and mourns their losses.
- I desire friends who operate from a place of acceptance as opposed to performance.
- I want a relational environment free of manipulation and ulterior motives.

- I desire fulfilling working relationships, win-win scenarios, and team-based environments.
- I want a group of people who are consistent in action, word, and character.
- I want relationships with those who call out, believe, and fight for the best in others.

Now I realize these might seem like lofty goals, but this is the actual direction my relational life is headed. It's not to say I have everything I want relationally, but it means I steward people with my wants in mind. This has taken pressure off my relationships, which in turn gives me more of the health I want. As I went into interactions having already established my immediate intent and motivation (be about others first) and my relational desires (healthy and whole friendships), a fun thing started to happen. I was then able to widely invest in and love others without expectation because it's simply who I chose to be. That desire to invest in others did not then mean each person I met or engaged with was brought into the inner sanctum of my relational world. Not everyone plays the same role in our lives. But when I *did* meet people I wanted to get to know, being other-focused meant I already had relational equity in the bank with them. Knowing what we want in relationships and what is nonnegotiable for us helps create healthy boundaries to operate within.

Pulling the Weeds

Knowing what we *don't* want in our relationships can be as useful as knowing what we *do* want. Before we continue, I'd like to define two unhealthy relational behaviors, so you understand exactly what I mean. Of course, there are more, but these two I find especially problematic. In the end, genuinely toxic behaviors can lead to larger and more damaging behaviors to sort out later.

You might quickly glance ahead and notice I've placed "continual" in front of each behavior. I say this to point out that I am not making difficult behavior but the continual employment of and unwillingness to grow beyond unhealth the enemy. So although I may still encounter these behaviors from time to time, in those I love and in myself, they are much more like an odd weed or patch of dead grass that needs to be plucked than an entire lawn filled with dandelions and dry sod.

Continual manipulation looks like passive-aggressive communication, indirect requests, and guilt or shame as tools used to get desired results, conversations, or relational investment. Manipulation is a symptom of control and a stone's throw from abusive behavior. *Example: Your friend finds out you're going to do something they'd like to be invited or included in. A direct way of addressing this would be to say something like, "Hey, I heard you're doing ____ and truthfully, that sounds like a blast. Would there be any way I could join? Genuinely no pressure if not." But manipulation takes a different route. A friend using manipulation might start texting you in the morning asking what you're up to, trying to vaguely catch up or get life updates. Then they hit you with, "What do you have going tonight? I'd love to see you." What you may or may not have realized is that you've been backed into offering an invitation or withholding it, a decision that will no doubt be added to or subtracted from your relational account in that person's eyes. This is the starting point of dangerous relational dynamics that yield messy results if unattended.*

Continual lying is a consistent disregard for the truth, regardless of perceived "importance." Lying is a symptom of insecurity and, when unattended to, leads to a lack of conviction, indecisiveness, and an inability to make decisions that genuinely propel one forward in life.

Example: Someone continually retells stories and conversations with real inaccuracy, lies about scores in sports or games, "doesn't remember" saying something hurtful, or exhibits gaslighting behavior through phrases like, "No, I wasn't mean; you're just sensitive. I didn't yell; I just got excited." They may as well tell you the sky isn't blue.

Although we are not immune to self-serving behaviors, establishing some boundaries in our lives of what we want and what we're trying to steer clear of will keep us moving forward in health. If we think of our relational environments like a garden bed, I'd liken applying boundaries to our lives to be a sort of pruning. Go with me on this, because you know I love a metaphor. By prioritizing the qualities that serve us and our relationships (healthy plants, flowers, and vegetables) and limiting the qualities that don't (weeds and dead or rotten branches), we're exponentially increasing the health of our relationship environments—our own "garden beds."

As I hope you've gathered, I'm not trying to get out of loving and liking people. However, there have been a handful of friendships in my life that have not traveled the distance I thought they would. This is no indictment on any person. Life can shift relational dynamics simply based on circumstances and a number of other outside factors. Add to that physical location and behaviors and intent that may be at odds with one another's trajectories, and friendly and communal relationships become tricky to navigate.

Regardless, know that you have every right to a healthy relational life that supports and rallies behind you. It is not idyllic or naive to say that you can have a healthy and solid network of people who function, behave, and love exactly as they seem. No, it might not happen overnight, and it might require actual work, but you are not stuck where you are.

So the question becomes, what will you do next?

Partnership Matters

Have you ever thought about what the company you keep says about you? You may have heard this sentiment from a parental figure, or from society at large. I'd like to take it a step further and say that the company you keep has the power to make relational inroads or blockades for you. I'm not talking about networking; I'm not talking about being surrounded with the "right" kind of people, the ones who have the most sizzling personalities, the ones who are quick to validate you, the ones who have a measure of success you want. I want you to have a relational environment that brings a level of tangible life and oxygen to you. You deserve to be around people who are as invested in others as you are.

I want to encourage you to surround yourself with those who are willing to similarly leave the comfort of their own priorities and agendas to meet you where your needs are. If I spur on a level of selfless awareness in you and tell you that you have to be the only selflessly motivated one in your life, I would be setting you up for an exhausting life.

A wonderful side effect of prioritizing selflessness, astute thoughtfulness, and empathy is that you will find others with your same motivation. One of my favorite things to notice in any room is "Where are the thoughtful ones?" It could be that I trip, and I look up to see who else saw and shares a laugh with me—even that tells me a person is aware of their environment. When there aren't enough seats for a group, and I catch someone "clock" that and immediately get up to find one or offer their own? That's a person I'll always want to meet. Maybe I'm in a business meeting and I notice one person engages a question a bit more than they normally would because the other person is enjoying the conversation or feels it important. Because my sight line goes beyond the topical, I look for those with a similar sight line. And guess what? I find them. When thoughtful people are around each other, they'll recognize each other and begin building relational trust more quickly.

We have a finite amount of energy to give out. That energy, as we've talked about, can be invested, donated, and exchanged, but it can also be taken. So although we've talked about meeting people we encounter where they are with what we have available, I'm not asking you to marry every person or invite each acquaintance into a deep friendship. I'm not asking you to make each person at work your best friend or to even spend copious amounts of time with each person who crosses your path. Right where you are, with what you have—that's what I'm asking you for.

When you see a person consistently lose their cool when someone questions their opinion, you're most likely going to be less interested in sharing your thoughts with that person or having them heavily involved in your life contributing theirs. If you see someone cruelly make fun of someone else, you're going to be less likely to feel safe having that person in intimate circles. If you see someone make a mess in the break room and leave it for someone else to clean up, you might feel less inclined to have that person over for dinner. And guess what? That's fair.

This isn't to say you should disregard those who don't seem aligned with your goals, but to simply keep your eyes open and up, looking for those exercising characteristics you want to see more of in your life.

Because your partnerships speak on your behalf, they can make your relational life easier or harder. If you've been in a long-term relationship, I know you'll understand this. When you're with someone who genuinely considers others, your relational world and possibilities therein exponentially increase. This makes me think of a married couple who are also some of my closest friends. The husband and I had already been friends, and he had already been thoughtful before their marriage. When he met his bride, it was like he met an accelerant to his own life. She not only came into the relationship ready to partner with him, she came into it wanting to empower, expand, and build on to an already beautiful life he'd established. She did this by bridging relational gaps in his family and friends as they arose, investing in his world with genuine love, and loving far beyond herself and without a need for reciprocation or approval. She garnered trust in his world as she securely and thoughtfully handled those in his life and her own. Because of her tangible investment, she immediately had the same equity he did in his life, and he in hers. She chose to walk out her intentionality with others and to truly partner with his life, not diminish or change it. She was a true teammate. Before too long, their combined work ethic, thoughtfulness, and intentionality with those in their lives exponentially propelled them into more of their own fulfilled dreams of work, family, and overall joy. Because of how well both my friends have invested in each other's lives, they have one of the most defined and beautiful unions I've seen. The truth? That didn't just happen. That was fought for with intentionality, real love, and a genuine willingness to lean out of self and into another.

On the other hand, selfish or somewhat thoughtless partners can isolate you from the relational world you want. Now, why is that? Because their actions will eventually speak to your character and build a narrative that communicates on your behalf. After all, we're talking about a *partnership*, right? It's not just you and it's not just them contributing to the relational atmosphere you live in. You might be one of the most selfless and joy-filled people in the world, but if your husband or wife, your business partner, or closest friend is primarily focused on themself and their conquests, that disconnect will show up down the road and create a ceiling to the shared relational depth you can experience with that person.

Has someone you were incredibly close to ever married someone you didn't quite trust or feel wholly safe to speak freely around? You might not trust that person immediately or sense that they're somewhat dishonest, or you might not be convinced of their intent to be purely selfless in dealing with your loved one . . . or your loved one's loved ones. When this happens, the relational fractures surrounding the loved one might be hairline at first, but they'll soon have far-reaching effects, like the potential of any unattended crack in a foundation or windshield.

Let's look at either side of this so you can see clearly what I mean. Let's say your hypothetical friend Corinne just started dating a new guy, Quincy. Corinne is just the best. She really cares about the people she encounters; she isn't overly extroverted and doesn't need to be the "life of the party." She has a quiet confidence and deep love for others. Quincy, on the other hand, is a great time.

He's extroverted and funny, aware of a room and how he can work it. He's an impressively entertaining person, but he doesn't care to know anyone in Corinne's life beyond a surface level and generally likes to talk about himself. Fairly tolerable as offenses go, to begin with at least. But as they continue dating, maybe you notice Quincy's selfish behavior has expanded to other areas. Maybe now he's regularly cutting Corinne off so he can speak; maybe he's shooting down different viewpoints or perspectives in the room; maybe he's become quick to frustration.

Let me ask you a question. Would Quincy's marriage to your friend excite you? Chances are they wouldn't. In fact, there's a greater chance your friend's choice of spouse would lead to a disconnect between you and your friend down the road. I'm not saying it's irreparable; I'm not saying I haven't seen friends who don't like each other's spouses figure out a friendship. I am, however, saying that I've seen people I adore lose intimacy and trust in their relationships because of the spouse with whom they chose to align. When we see someone we love partner with someone who is counter to their relational culture, it's like a 747 flying with two engines throttled at 100 percent and the other two 100 percent thrusted in reverse. It's difficult to move toward any relational growth with such an opposition.

Your parents? They're meant to stick by you regardless of who you choose.

Everyone else? They get a choice.

You? You get a choice.

Styling your life is as much about an ability to choose as it is an ability to cut out bad behaviors and form ones better suited for how you move through life. The qualities of the relational fabric we choose to dress in may be the basis of our outfit, but those qualities we align and walk with most intimately are like the jewelry, neckties, cuff links, and shoes that complete that outfit. Relational priorities and intent make up our outfit, and the ways in which we *show* those priorities and intent are the accessories that bring it all together.

A bright paisley tie paired with a muted plaid suit? Rough.

Incredibly fitted and cut gown with muddy sneakers on? Not the look.

So then what? If you find yourself in the middle of a relational atmosphere you'd like to see changed, know that it can be changed. I'm not asking you to dump those you love by the wayside on your journey to "health." That's not healthy at all. However, you can invite people to meet you in healthy behaviors that support relationships by simply prioritizing those behaviors in your life.

PUTTING IT INTO PRACTICE: **Frameworkers**

As you begin to build the sort of relational world you truly want to invest in and withdraw from, there are some ways to begin moving toward your own styled life—right now. Like marking the boundaries on a new plot of land, you can create the floor plan of your relational world. Here are some *frameworkers*, or foundational principles, to help you do this:

- Identify one friend or person whose relational world you respect. Have a conversation with them and ask what qualities they value in those they're closest to.
- Take some personal inventory of your own social circle and identify one way to contribute health where it's lacking. Then bring it to the table. Maybe you and your friends are used to gossiping about others. Next time you can feel a conversation going that way, curb it by complimenting or calling attention to something you respect, admire, or appreciate about the person. If your family isn't great at celebrating others, bring that to the table yourself with some simple acknowledgments and teach your family how to get excited for others without *teaching* them.
- Establish a boundary without needing to have a conversation about it. If you work a typical nine-to-five job and have not explicitly been asked nor agreed to answer emails on the weekend, log off your email Friday after

work. If something pressing does come up that's not a true emergency, you can simply say, "I'll be happy to address this Monday morning. Have a great weekend." Part of successfully working in a job you love is loving yourself enough to establish healthy working boundaries within it. It gives you respect and longevity in the business, and shows that you value time—yours and everyone else's.

- Recognize someone with a quality you would like to have more of in your life and make a tangible effort to invest in a friendship. I'm not saying you buy matching shirts as a gift. Instead, be decisive and ask to take them to lunch; if you know some places they especially enjoy, possibly offer those up. You could even take them for a drink after work someday or ask them to join you and your friends for an already planned activity. Just think of a next step you can take to keep the relational ball in the air.

As this shift in personal operating strategy happens, we move into daily giving away the health we choose for ourselves. It's in the everyday things, in the small but consistent rhythm of giving away our empathy, awareness, and tangible engagement, that we begin to live as leaders in our lives. It's in our ability and willingness to have hard conversations that don't sear another's heart, in our quickness to own our own selfishness-sullied contributions, where change actually happens, when we continually choose to step up and into more real maturity.

9

Everyday Giveaway

GENEROSITY DOESN'T START WITH HAVING money, an initiative, a program, research dollars, or immediate answers—those are just delivery systems for generosity. It doesn't begin with a social media rant guilting others into action either, just in case you were wondering. Generosity itself can be found, or found lacking, in the posture of how we live and how we lean out of ourselves. More literally, it's in the readiness with which we're willing to give. As you've now seen, I relate much of how we live to the physical world . . . which is ironic. I'm not the most physically coordinated or spatially aware person. In fact, it requires real effort on my part to be mindful of my physicality. Now does that mean I consistently am? Just ask the side table between my bathroom and kitchen that I run into weekly. It hasn't moved in five years, although I'm sure it wishes it could.

However, I've learned I move differently when I simply take a moment to take account of my surroundings. It's only when I stop engaging and switch on my cruise control that I run into poles mid-conversation. (No, that's not a hypothetical. Yes, I've actually done that two times, years apart, if we're being honest. Fool me twice, huh?) I'd like to say I'm less of a relational klutz, but left on cruise control, I can be just as callous and unaware as I am physically banging into a corner I think I can clear without trying.

As we explore the generosity available to us in how we engage others, let's understand that our generosity is first defined by the readiness of our posture, not by what we're holding in our hand as we lean out. It's as simple as a shift of weight. It's like going from sitting slouched back in a seat to sitting up with your weight grounded in your heels. I think about rush hour in NYC and crowded trains—you'll never catch me fully relaxed or sitting back taking a nap. There's way too much going on and the environment you're in changes with every stop. A peaceful train car can instantly become a performance space, a boxing ring, a sing-along, a yelling match, and so much more. What enables me or anyone else to navigate these various situations is staying ready, staying engaged, and being ready to move. Although my motivation for staying alert underground is partly for my safety, I can apply the principle to generosity and use the same readiness in my relationships. Trains, living rooms—it doesn't matter the environment. It matters that we're ready to meet others and the needs they may have—and with a flexibility to do so in whatever way is needed.

Now that we've journeyed together as far as we have, you can probably see that the principles we've highlighted so far have been priming us all for a posture change. I've been stretching out some muscles for us we might not be used to exercising. As leaders—those who desire to foster growth in the lives of others and in their immediate communities—we can only achieve that change by starting with us, with our own flexibility. To move from passively existing in our lives to actively contributing to the lives and atmospheres we touch means going from sitting back in the chair of your life to leaning forward, ready to move, adjust, get up quickly, or sit back down for the sake of another.

I'm not talking about living like a runner on the blocks or like a ball girl or ball boy at a tennis match. Like we discussed in the last chapter, to operate as you're meant to be means not just trying to help others out of some pressure to do so. It means that we, standing flat-footed in who we've decided to be, are able to reach out and give of ourselves at astonishing levels. That's because your generosity and mine will look as different as we are. I'm not trying to replicate anyone else's sight line, nor would I ever want you to. But with any fortune, your generosity and my generosity might meet in the same room someday. Together, like teammates, we'd join our kindness, empathy, and ability to read and understand the room together, advocating for the people there while we do it. A football team isn't solely made up of quarterbacks, kickers, or a defensive line—it's varied, and each member serves in the ways they're especially skilled to move the ball down the field.

My life and experiences have equipped me to speak from my vantage point and not yours, and vice versa. I say that to release any pressure you might feel to be someone you're not. You're meant to be the fullest version of yourself wherever you are and, from that place, you are meant to lean out and add where you're able—relationships, environments—with the tools you have.

You may be reading this thinking, *This feels a little out of reach and I don't quite know where to begin.* Wonderful, that's a great place to start. Maybe take account of what you already have to give away each day and start there. It might be that you're a quiet person who doesn't feel like they're the most social. You still have a kind smile to give, you might have an extra pen or piece of gum to offer someone on your commute, a hand to offer that woman trying to lift her luggage, or an extra bottle of water to offer that runner you pass every day, or you might have a sincere compliment you've been holding in. "I love the questions you ask. You've got a great mind." I realize that isn't something we're used to "throwing around," but, friend, get used to throwing yourself into just a little bit of discomfort to vulnerably offer yourself up and (here it comes again) lean out. In this vulnerability, you won't always be met with those who receive your intent with open arms or those who understand where you're coming from, and that's okay. Go ahead and take the pressure of another's response off your plate. That's not your concern.

Regardless of where each of us is in life, we have the ability to activate our generosity where it's easiest for us. This gets us used to the rhythm of living with our *eyes up* and hands out of our pockets. In my life, I've come to know the tools and relational resources I have to use and give out at will, but that wasn't something I woke up one morning already knowing. I started with what was most easily available to me. When I first started living into my gifts, all I really knew about myself was that I could make people laugh and I could encourage most people. So I started there. At that point, I had jokes, quips, and comments ready to go. I made it my mission to leave the room a bit brighter than when I had entered. But that was just the start.

So think about where you're most at home in yourself—that's the best place to begin. To illustrate this, I'd like to brag about one of my nearest and dearest. He's a guy my age who has just worked incredibly hard. I have watched him closely over the last decade, and he has built quite an impressive career for himself. He's an incredibly successful music producer and songwriter who often works six days a week and has limited free time. Most weeks he's only really able to hang out for an evening or two, as his schedule is insane. However, insane schedule, Grammy nominations, and Billboard number ones aside, he is without a doubt the most kind and gentle man, especially with others trying to reach any measure of his success in their own careers. He has always been generous with his time, with his advice, and with his encouragement.

But as his career began to be more public-facing and his songs started climbing the charts, what he had developed in relational strength was now matched—and made even brighter—by his wins within the industry. His talent, work ethic, and consistency as well as the way he treats others combine to make a truly solid person of integrity, and he's respected as such.

Now, the person everyone knew to be kind, willing to listen to their issues and give loving and nonjudgmental encouragement, willing to listen to their songs, and willing to chat about music and to lament about the industry's woes, was a bona fide hitmaker. He had steered his craft in conjunction with the equity he built with people to such an extent that when he did become successful on paper, the respect he'd always commanded exponentially grew. Humility is one of the most promotable qualities. Possession of it speaks to a person's willingness to own their mistakes, be teachable in a role, and be mindful of existing gaps (relationally or within a system); it speaks to a comprehensive, outward-oriented awareness and not an inflated, self-focused one. A humble person who then excels at what they do all *while* treating people well sees exponential wins.

My friend was always generous. He still is. Whether it was food, drink, a couch to crash on, a listening ear, industry insight, or a connection to a potential collaborator (when it made sense), it didn't matter. If he had it, he was willing to give it to you. No doubt, if you were to walk into a big group, you would see my friend in the corner deep in a conversation, giving every bit of himself. Because he's successful on paper, people want his opinion and time, sure. I understand that. But because of the quality and authenticity of his lean out and the way he subsequently leans in, he commands a level of respect he's never had to ask for. His life and character house his success and not the other way around. And because of how he's chosen to handle others, he has a village of people cheering him on in his ascent. His level of giving wasn't dependent on his success. He gave right where he was with what he had, whenever able. He still does.

I realize we're not all cool music producers and that many of us don't necessarily feel as passionately in pursuit of our dreams as I know him to be. That's not the point. It's the same kindness I saw in his and his wife's lovely one-bedroom apartment, where I crashed on the bed in the living room, as I see now in their beautiful home. His success is in alignment with who he's always been, and now he is a quite realized version of himself, fully in the middle of his stance and simultaneously ready to jump or pivot to what's next. He might be finishing a song or encouraging a friend today. Either way and whatever's up next, I can tell you he's ready for it.

My question: Are *you* ready to move from where you are?

If I'm leaning against a wall with my hands firmly in the pockets of my coat and someone trips in front of me, dropping their phone or grocery bag, I'm less ready to meet them in a moment. But if I'm in the center of my stance with arms free, I'm able to move in any direction at that moment. Living in a rhythm of generosity is no different. It requires us to get our hands out of our pockets, no matter where we are. It requires us being available in the spaces where we exist, to not only help but contribute.

In fine-tuning how we see the world around us, in seeing beyond the surface of a moment or situation into the reality of what a person may be experiencing, we've set ourselves up for this new posture of generosity. Plus, as you'll recall, we have a ton of new tools available to help us do this.

Tool Roll Call

Let's take some inventory together. So far, we have learned to navigate relational dynamics with genuine awareness. With empathy as our lens, we've learned how to genuinely survey an atmosphere and those in it, acting based on what we see and sense; we've understood how meeting others' immediate needs is an investment that pays off in the long run. Then we dove into conflict resolution, handling the gnarly people-moments of life and walking out of those fires with relational equity intact, if not grown. Realizing how powerful and important the addition of tangible empathy is to our lives, we learned it should be in how we speak, how we behave, and how we think of others. Then we took this awareness out of the abstract and into concrete action; after that we moved into a discussion of what we want our relational lives to look like.

And here's the connection I want you to see. Each healthier relational principle, each time you move toward being more aware of another than you are of yourself, each thoughtful and measured conversation you have when all you want to do is react, each kind and edifying thing you can say about a coworker, mutual friend, or family member moves you closer to being alive with intentionality and thoughtfulness. This, in turn, makes you a room-reading stakeholder and contributor wherever you go. After all, these are tools of tangible generosity. However, there really are countless ones available to you.

So let's talk about some tools you have available right now where you are.

You have the tools to connect empathy with an action that clearly communicates that empathy (chapters three, four, five, and nine).

Now, in caring about another and truly leaning into the world around you to know where someone is or where they might be coming from, you can take small and immediate action to meet them in your leaning out of yourself.

Example: Your child's Little League coach is there long before practice starts and well after it's done. You might conclude, "I can tell he's exhausted and see him yawning through practice; I know he works a day job, too. It's been slow at my work lately, so I'm going to come to practice early and leave a little later to help him set up and clean up."

You have the tools to meet immediate needs when you're looking for them (chapters one, two, six, and nine).

By truly adjusting your eyes to the world around you, you can see the immediate needs of others and meet them.

Example: You've just gone out for drinks with some of your friends and everyone's laughing, hugging, and trying to order all at once. While you wait for a break in the conversation, you notice a guy talking awfully close to a woman who looks less than comfortable. In a matter of seconds, you see her try to brush him off multiple times but he only tries harder. You might wait until you're sure danger is clear, or you might immediately walk over (maybe bring a friend) and open with something like, "Girl, we're over here. How did you not see us? I'm sorry, sir, but she's with her friends tonight." Get her out of the immediate ick and then ask her, "Are you okay and is there anything we can do to make sure you feel safe? Is there someone you're meeting or do you want to hang with us?" You know, be normal and caring.

You have the tools to respond to a whole person as opposed to reacting to a single behavior (chapters three and four).

When you learn the cost of your reaction and instead take hold of your responses, you end up bringing needed balance to an uncomfortable interaction.

Example: Your coworker just had an intense meeting with their oversight and was blamed for a whole shipment of equipment not going out. When you see them an hour later, they are clearly in a bad mood. They make a comment to the effect of, "I don't know why you didn't get into trouble, too; it's both our account and Jeff [oversight] knows it." A reaction might say, "Well, my job is to compile every piece and get it to the shipping department. Your job is to make sure it gets shipped." A response might be, "I'm sorry you had that rough conversation. I'm sure it didn't feel great. You're right, this is both our account so let's you and I get together at the end of the week and see how I can better help set you up for success. Do you have an hour in your schedule where we could talk through it?"

You have the ability to look at patterns and intuit a corresponding response (chapters three, four, and six).

In being genuinely observant you will learn what makes people tick. You'll see what they love and can't stomach, the ways they like being talked to, and the ways that they don't. You'll learn their preferences in everyday things such as food, drinks, and music. Watch a person more closely and you'll even see the types of people they attract, the sort they're able to hear hard things from, the ones they don't respect, and the ones they really love. In taking in information, we amass data patterns that show paths to relational success. *Example: I know my boss consistently has meetings on Wednesdays and Thursdays that drain her. So I'm not only going to save my big questions for Monday, Tuesday, and Friday, if possible; I'm going to make sure I'm checking in on her "draining days" to see what I can do to help. If she says nothing, I'm just going to consistently stop by her office once a week and remind her I'm here if she needs anything.*

Example: In a conversation with your spouse, you notice they are beginning to spiral over a comment made to them during the workday, school pickup line, on the basketball court, wherever. Because you've learned they often internalize and give credence to unhealthy comments made by others, you've learned to replace the incomplete narrative with the truth you see. After all, you're watching now. Really watching. You might just say, "I'm so glad you told me and I'm so sorry that cruel thing was said. But because I love you, I can't let you think their perspective is our reality. I see you as thorough, settled, loving, competent . . ." Thanks to you recognizing a pattern in them, you now have the ability to take the hurtful thorns of life out before they infect and fester.

You have the tools to serve up real solutions based on understanding you've gained (chapters seven and nine).

Your awareness of the environment and people around you has given you the ability to bridge major divides. Your empathy allows you to see people outside your personal bias, and tying action to that empathy allows you deeper access to those in your orbit.

Example: Let's say your group of friends is having an issue. Two parties are in real disagreement. One of them just stopped engaging with the group the way they used to. Maybe they've gone from being plugged in to hanging out, checking in with you, and pursuing relationships with the group to just disappearing for a time. Because you've been clued in on them empathetically, you know they're really struggling to find footing in their life. One of your friends just got engaged, another just married, one's having a baby, and most of them are in jobs they love. Life has repeatedly knocked this friend down, and they're doing what they can to show up, but they're having a hard time. Your friends who are less clued in might get mad and hurt. "I can't believe they've just disappeared. It's like they don't even care about us." Because you know more, you can build a bridge.

"I know it feels like they don't care. But it's possible they might be in the middle of navigating a lot of big life changes. You know they lost a parent two years ago and don't talk about it. They got laid off at the job they loved when cuts had to be made. They're back at ground zero having to build up from there. I know it's easy to be angry, because it's frustrating, but maybe we should lean in to meet them. Can we each take turns calling and reminding them we love them and want to have a fun dinner soon? Who cares if they don't respond for a month? It's probably a bit hard for them to see and feel everyone they love is in their mountaintop moments while they're trudging through what feels like a valley. So let's give them some grace and a lot of love. Any other ideas you have to meet them where they are?"

These tools are just the starting point. Only you'll know what's needed in your specific environments. This level of thoughtfulness will deepen and strengthen relationships in your life tangibly.

Our lives are complex, and they come with an awful lot to navigate. Having a healthy culture around us, marked by selfless awareness and real empathy, only supports our navigation. But if we don't have that culture, it's up to us to build it, piece by piece. If I have an incredibly unhealthy working environment, guess whose job it is to bring fresh water to that culture, even if I only work in the mail room? You guessed it: mine.

I don't have to march into the CEO's office talking about how inefficient the working environment is. I can simply do my job with an added layer of empathy and begin leading myself and others from where I am to engage our empathetic muscles by unflinching example. Then sometime down the road, if I feel the need to address something on a larger scale, I've already laid the groundwork to do so. Do you have a gossipy environment you're trying to change? Stop engaging in gossip. In fact, nothing kills a gossipy environment faster than one person who doesn't want to talk ill of others. Maybe you want to start seeing more teamwork. So instead of solely focusing on your own tasks, offer contributions elsewhere where you see them possible. Know that you have tools to use so that you're not just existing in a given space. You are a stakeholder and MVP positioned for upward movement.

Let's Talk Branding

I recently spent a little time with a globally respected founder and billionaire. I say that only to showcase that the following principle is absolutely tied to her and her business's success. She was talking about the visual branding of her company. They had very specific colors from the beginning, an aesthetic all their own, and a great logo. She explained that one cannot underestimate the importance of brand recognition—that it creates a throughline that customers and potential customers will come to rely on, whether or not they realize it. She talked about having their logo on shirts, towels, pens, coffee cups, laptop stickers, and on and on. As I listened to her, I saw my own throughline from her explanation to you, reader, right now.

Although you and I have access to the same relational tools, we'll grab for different ones. For instance, as you lean into this selfless side of you, you might find yourself to be incredibly gifted in bringing order to chaos. You might be wonderful at organizing things, period, helping people connect dots where they haven't before, bringing clarity to confusion, and more. If that's the case, then your "branding" lies in clarity, order, and reliability. Where you're able and where it makes sense, how can you communicate that branding? You might be like one of my nearest and dearest friends . . . she always leaves a space slightly tidier and more together than it was when she found it, even if it's simply straightening loose papers on a table. It's not out of anxiety or some "need to," but she, without calling attention to it or making a fuss, will adjust, reorganize, or refocus an area of chaos (even an in-store display) to leave it genuinely better. That's very much who she is, and because she regularly cultivates that "branded" side of herself, she's able to easily exercise it without breaking a sweat. The qualities you regularly cultivate are the ones you'll be able to exercise without stressing your relational muscles.

As we grow in our careers and relationships, those qualities we regularly cultivate and give away in passing interactions or in quiet moments are the equivalent of giving out a nice branded pen or laptop sticker (for instance, one that says "Order"). While not the entirety of your brand, these consistent parts of you reveal how you want to be known. And when you've leaned out and into others, even in small interactions, they then walk around marked by your influence. As opportunity makes its way to preparation and moments of promotion in life come, the branded investment you've made in people's lives rises up to speak on your behalf. Nothing stays hidden, especially not a pure intention.

Then, people begin connecting that brand of selflessness to the kind thing you said, to the big project you saved the day on, to the time you brought your brother dinner for a week because he couldn't kick the flu, and to you comprehensively. In other words, you have *brand integrity*. Well, integrity, period.

We don't know when we'll be given an opportunity to give out our pens and stickers, so it's best to just live ready to reach for one. Everybody loves a good pen, right?

However, I remember a night I was less than ready to dole out stickers. A couple years ago I was at dinner with some friends, and we somehow ended up collecting about fifteen more people at our table. Now between you and me, I really don't enjoy being surprised by big groups. But since life is hilarious, I find myself in this situation often. I'll think I'm going to dinner with two friends, and it ends up being six, sometimes fifteen. I've become much more flexible in life, but it's still not my preference. But remember, regardless of my personal dislike for being in large groups of people forced to make small talk, my preferences are not the first thing that inform my behavior. If that were the case, I wouldn't be very kind. So, at this particular dinner, as the table began to grow, I decided to lean in, engage, and have fun with it. I was being separated from the very people I came to spend time with, and although it's an opportunity to be irritated, it's also an opportunity to engage.

There was a couple from the other group who found themselves looking for seats and for some reason, the wife made eye contact with me and told her husband they were coming to sit by me. I must've had one of those "sit by me; I won't bite" faces. As the woman threw the train of her gown behind her as she sat down, she did not give me a "hello," "hi," or even a "I'm ____; it's nice to meet you." She exhaled as she took her seat, turned her head to me, and said directly into my eyes, "My daughter hates me. I don't know why I felt like I was supposed to tell you that, but it's the truth and I needed to say it." Well, that's quite a lead-in, right? I took a breath and realized, *Oh, I get it, this is where I'm meant to contribute tonight.*

We talked for a while over a breakdown she and her daughter had, some relational hurdles she felt she was having to jump over daily, mistakes she'd made in parenting and how she worried she'd be paying for them the rest of her life. It was heavy. Although her husband was in *schmooze* mode, as drinks were being ordered, laughter and stories shared all around us, she was in a hopeless place, quietly crying and leaning close to tell me about her breaking heart. The juxtaposition between a person mentally free-falling while at a "party" is the reality we live in daily. I just got to see this reality unobscured by subtlety. It was unmissable. I know I'm not a therapist, so when these conversations come my way, I try to help in immediate ways—small wins. No, I'm not trained to be able to walk back the dysfunction created in a whole family over dinner and drinks. I'd often like to. But instead, we had a very honest conversation wherein I was able to give her some actionable items that made her feel less powerless. "Let your daughter be mad right now. I would be. You dropped the ball as a mom and she needs to know you know it. Work through this all with a therapist and not with her. She's not responsible for how you're doing or feeling about you messing up. Kill any expectations you have of her and simply show up in her world, fully about her and unattached from your own need to make things better for you. If you want a new relationship, begin new relational patterns."

Now, having said all that, let me bring some balance. I did not camp out with my new friend all night working through her family drama. She did not take over my night. Now, possibly seven or eight years ago I would have offered up my night to her willingly. But learn from me and know that this was one of the first nights I remember intentionally saying to myself, *Yes, I can pour into this person and give some perspective to encourage her. I have it to give, so let me give it. But I'm also not going to be pinned in a corner all night with someone I didn't intentionally come to spend quality time with.* So after about twenty minutes of working through this situation, I simply said, "It's been so nice chatting with you and I know you and your daughter are going to have a different relationship than you've had, because I know you truly want it. Now just take some steps. Have a great one." And then I walked to the other side of the table and pulled up a chair by my friends to continue our evening. Remember, it would be false for me to have stayed in her situation, giving up my night to help her sort a relational problem far above my paygrade. Because I only gave the insight I felt I was supposed to, what I was willing to, and what made sense in the moment, I rang true and with authority. This further established my brand and a bit of brand loyalty from the few people listening to that conversation, the mom included.

Every day, regardless of what our environment looks like, we have the opportunity to give away something of ourselves without fear of it being lost to us because we gave it. It cost me nothing but some time and focused energy to be able to leave that woman better than she was when she moped over to me. It did not deplete my ability or desire to care about others; it didn't cost me money; it merely cost me effort and intention. Those are renewable resources. The more you sense in a person or room, the more you make yourself available and act on what you can with what you have available to you—the more you speed up the metabolism of your generosity.

Brick by Brick

What I hope you're realizing at this point is that each chapter in this book has been like a brick. And just like bricks are laid upon one another to build a whole structure, the concepts we've covered so far have been intended for you to gradually increase your self-awareness, your capacity to lean out of yourself and into others no matter where you are. You'll notice many of my examples are based in relational spaces and somewhat unique social environments. Because of my life and where it's taken me, I've had the ability to grow a great amount of focused skills to contribute *where I* am. Now if I loved Major League Baseball, working and functioning in that world, the skills I would need relationally might look different on the surface, although the intent is the same. That's why you have to clue in to where *you* are, the culture at play around you, and learn to speak to *that* environment. You don't have to be a tenured teacher to contribute to the health of the community in a faculty. However, for you to be impactful to that culture, you need to be settled enough in your own abilities and confidence therein to not dump your contribution where it's not wanted. That's like watering the concrete and being frustrated at the grass for not growing.

From a correctly motivated place, with understanding of your environment and how to contribute, you can intuit what's needed, know what you're able and willing to give, and give it genuinely. When you're able to contribute your generosity clearly and without the qualities of muddied purity, you can see life and health sprout and grow in your very backyard.

Think of your relational environment like a backyard with grass, concrete, a shed, a pool, and potted plants around. Please don't think I'm suggesting, as you stand on your back patio, that you drench everything you see with your relational contribution. You're not a water hose, and it would be wasteful to hydrate what cannot or doesn't need to be hydrated. Instead, think about carrying a large pitcher of water with you each day. That pitcher is filled with thoughtful questions, actual ability and insight to give away, and stories and history you're willing to share to connect with and make someone feel less alone. Speaking of myself, I have humor, an ability to see and notice what others often don't, skill sets that make me useful in business but also don't alienate me from creatives, and a desire and ability to leave others better off than I've found them. So that's the pitcher I leave home with each day. As my bandwidth and ability to grow myself increases, so does the size of my pitcher. Another word for that bandwidth is *capacity*. As your capacity grows, so does your contribution. In fact, it's this capacity that often allows successful CEOs and leaders of industry to be able to lead at such a high level without being overwhelmed.

Capacity. Let's see what ours is.

PUTTING IT INTO PRACTICE: Everyday Giveaways

Before we finally land this plane, I'd like to leave you with some *everyday giveaways* you can dole out daily and without much effort now that we're reorienting our vantage point. No fancy literary bait and switch here. It's not costly to give out of the character we've developed and the empathetic traits we've chosen to wear. Choose to make any of these a part of your day-to-day life and notice after some time the health, new growth, and calm that begins to develop in you and your relationships.

- Call one close friend or family member. Tell them you were just thinking about how grateful you are for them. Mean it. Ask them how they're doing, catch up for a bit, and then leave them encouraged. You can even decide what you'd like to leave them with before calling. You may be walking through a gnarly time in life but choose to focus on them. If they're sorting an issue or problem out, give them space to communicate it. If you have a way to help, do so. If you feel like you're supposed to tell them something, do so. But the point is to show up for someone without being asked.

- When someone says something you find especially insightful, funny, endearing, loving, generous, patient, thoughtful, or wonderful—tell them so, and then tell them why. Get used to being a well bubbling over with encouragement for others.
- Use the names of people you interact with in quick moments when possible. I know this isn't news for those *How to Win Friends and Influence People* fans, but I mean to speak someone's name like it's a gift to say. It can be someone working a box office with a name tag, a ride app driver or passenger, someone who works in maintenance at your building whose name you recently learned, the person checking you into your hotel, the older customer who routinely comes into your store; you get the idea. Just throw it on the end of a "hello" or "thank you," a "How are things, ___?" The point is to get used to immediately engaging with warmth and adding value to exchanges and the ones you have them with.
- If in a conversation or hang, you sense a misunderstanding is taking place—either you're being misunderstood

or doing the misunderstanding—initiate the resolution and begin the conversation by owning, and possibly apologizing for, any bit of your contribution to the issue.

With each action taken toward giving away some specific kindness, or simply giving yourself as a present person in a room, you will begin to know what I've been trying to impart since the first chapter. The bending, the cracking in your giving ligaments, the selflessness that's now entering your bloodstream like a rush of fresh oxygen, it's all going to reveal a physiological principle you're accepting in your heart and in the way you engage with people: you're made to be flexible, to bend.

10

Meant to Bend

IN THE LATE 1980S IN Oracle, Arizona, construction began on a heralding experiment. It was a research facility called Biosphere 2 and comprised seven different and completely enclosed biomes (savanna, rainforest, ocean, fog desert, agricultural area, wetlands, and a human habitat). Scientists designed these biomes to be completely self-sufficient and to function together as a sort of micro Earth. The goal was to see if these biomes, along with eight people and plenty of animals, could be completely self-sustainable: a potential future model for living in space. They grew their own food and lived like scientists on another planet. In a completely controlled environment, they had to figure out the creation of oxygen, water, food, and the disposal of everything in between. It all had to happen in the biosphere. The experiment ran twice, the first time for exactly two years (1991 to 1993) and the second only for ten months in 1994 because the mission, although impressive, had its fair share of challenges.

Psychological dynamics between the residents of Biosphere 2 became volatile after two years, with a low caloric intake and dropping oxygen levels partly to thank. In the end, the low morale, relational discord, and fatigue were not dissimilar to what might have been experienced by a crew returning from a space mission. Although this experiment is shrouded in controversy due to several miscalculations that made the biosphere challenging to sustain, I find one discovery to be particularly illuminating. The trees they had planted in the constructed environment couldn't mature. Scientists could get the trees to take root and they began growing easily, but they inevitably reached a literal breaking point. Their trunks simply couldn't sustain the weight of what they were growing. On the outside, an apple tree would look perfectly healthy but then reach a certain height and break in two.

Why was this? Biosphere 2, which had been engineered to create optimal conditions for growth, had neglected to account for the inherent obstacles that are essential to life and the sustained growth that leads to a fortified tree, plant, or animal. Sunshine and oxygen are crucial, yes—but so is wind. Trees need the resistance wind brings to mature and become durable enough to actually bolster and continue growth. Seedlings get their strength as they are made to bend and bow with the wind, not from avoiding the wind altogether.

Have you ever listened to the creaks and sounds of an old and seasoned tree? Although I wasn't very outdoorsy growing up, I love being out in nature. I especially love big trees and all the beauty and power they represent. More than that, I love the sounds they make. The way a breeze can move through different branches, hitting the leaves like some soothing chime; it's orchestral. Without fail, what

I am most arrested by each time is the way the newest and highest branches wildly wave and move in the wind, the way the settled supportive branches sway gracefully, as if dancing—it's my happiest place.

Then I often think about how old the tree must be. I think about the number of storms it's lived through, and, with each groan of the trunk, I think about the endless amount of bending the tree has been asked to do on account of the wind. If it couldn't move with the wind, it would be broken by it. A tree has to have great roots, but also an ability to shift. This is a tree that has been bent, formed in part, and made stronger by the wind pushing against it. And if a tree planted in one place for its entire existence is asked to hold its roots but still meet the wind, then you can meet your own gusts of wind: that difficult coworker, an angry person at the post office, a new group of friends with common ground you don't share, a foreign city you've just moved to, a potential spouse who has a completely different way of processing than you, a neighbor who staunchly disagrees with you and everything you believe, or a family member who's just always thought poorly of you. Wind takes all sorts of forms. Regardless of what the wind in your life looks like, you're meant to meet that gust and be a little bit stronger on the other side of it.

No, you're not a tree. You're far more complex with a great deal more strength, resilience, and ability to grow. You've more to offer than some shade, oxygen, and fruit every now and then. You've got a beating heart with emotions and sensitivities and unique qualities all your own.

However, not unlike a tree, you have a root system. Our experiences, influences, and belief systems deliver us (the tree) what we need to grow. Then we express that growth through how we lean out of ourselves in our abilities, the qualities we express, and the ways our characteristics grow and define—like branches extending in a beautiful silhouette.

Don't worry, you won't have to look for that resistance needed to grow. As you're living your life, storms of all sorts will meet you where you are. Whether it be the blustery wind of another person's trauma, the storm of an unhealthy environment, or the normal shifting breeze of a life filled with others, conflict is unavoidable. But without it, much like trees in a biodome free of resistance, we fail to mature. We can't even carry the weight of our own successes in life without snapping in two. Or worse, we produce what we're meant to in life, be it the "thing" we were supposed to build, the comprehensive work + life + love combination, or the skill we fine-tuned, and the weight of what we produce inevitably leads to our own breaking. Why? Because we didn't have the infrastructure to support all we were meant to produce.

At this point in our time together I hope to have provided you with empathetic tools that allow you to not only see others, but to meet them holistically. The desire has been to open your eyes to the actual relational world around you and equip you to meet it confidently and through a selflessly aware lens. This is not some vapid hypothesis of an idealistic world and how we ideally would meet each other in it.

This is real life. It's *your* real life. Every day, we encounter real people and real challenges, and we have the opportunity to come into those encounters with the very real tools we've collected.

While this is a book about meeting others, it's also a book about meeting yourself.

You're not a tree living in a shielded-from-real-life environment. You're not going to escape the wind that comes with people, I'm grateful to tell you. Because it's in the bending to understand another, in the shifting ebb and flow of relational dynamics, that we learn how to not be unmoved or unmoored by others, but to be flexible and, ultimately, stronger.

As seedlings grow alongside each other and withstand the winds and rain, learn to shift with them, and develop the root system needed to support their life, they change the landscape and create an ecosystem. This ecosystem ends up supplying life, protection, and sustainability to its land. That's what a community of healthy people looks like.

You're not some rogue pine tree on a mountain watching life happen beneath you. You've got "sequoia" written all over you.

Just like trees supply the land they inhabit with fresh oxygen, we provide fresh oxygen to situations we encounter. Acting when motivated by intuition, asking empathetic questions, mitigating disconnects where and when we can, changing the tone of a whole atmosphere by bringing a conversation back to its unemotional and main point—those are all exhales of oxygen. Oxygen is life and we have the power to give it to the relational worlds we exist in.

But will we?

You Got Something There

Trying to speak to people in your life—whether they be friends, coworkers, authority figures, or strangers you pass on the street—from a selfish core is like trying to tell someone off with snot falling out of your nose. You're welcome for the visual.

Now here's another image for you. Each time you begin a conversation with something you want to say or "need to" communicate, envision that inward-facing impulse like a rope tightly tied around you, immobilizing you. If you have to be a center point of the conversation, of your life, you will inadvertently end up tying yourself into inaction and isolation. Selfishness binds us in a straitjacket of our own making. That's because with every thought we cling to about how we're perceived, what we want, and how we can get it, we walk through life bound—by ourselves.

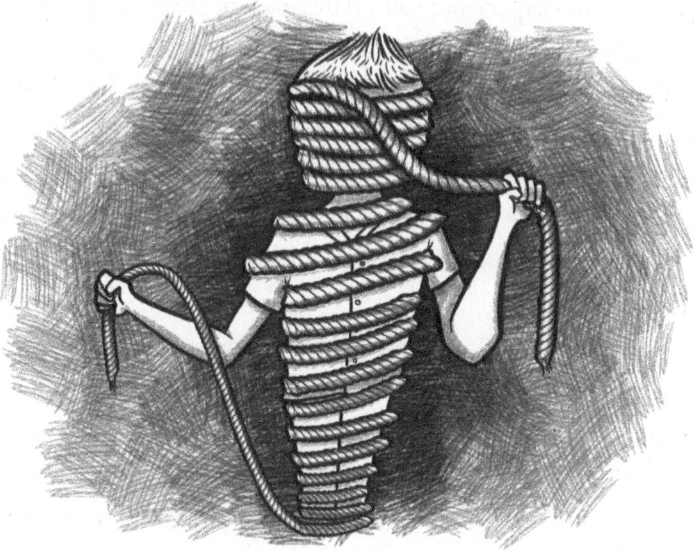

Selfishness changes everything that comes out of your mouth, like trying to speak through a rope your jaw is clenched around. Selfishness distorts communication and affects the integrity of any action or thought. Because if whatever you're doing or offering up is tied only to you and your benefit, you'll end up tying yourself down in the end.

Now I'd like for you to imagine having lived in such literal bondage for a number of years. Think about the way your body would be used to feeling in that stationary position. Never being able to fully extend the legs, arms, and even fingers of a body leads to mobility issues. Upon becoming untied, you might find it's a bit difficult to extend your legs the way you know they're meant to. Your arms and range of motion would be noticeably less and, with that, your overall strength. But let me ask you this: Is the limited mobility you'd experience caused by a lack of ability to grow muscle or the lack of growing muscle itself?

What concerns me most is not that we don't know how to get out of our selfishness; it's that we don't see a need to. Those whose selfless muscles have weakened over time have settled into a low-fi identity of "This is who I am now." But it's not who you are, and I love you enough to hold you accountable for information and insight you now have.

There are plenty of examples throughout our history when we learned something new and changed our behavior as a result. Take lead paint, for instance. Its uses were employed for centuries all over the world. And then we realized it was unhealthy, downright deadly. So what did we do? We stopped using it and started warning people of its presence.

That's the progression of humanity. As we learn more, we do better. We don't build houses the same way we did in the 1400s because we've learned more since then. Although each generation has built off the knowledge of the one before, each generation has not stayed in the same understanding of the generation before. We don't negate the principles that helped us discover and harness electricity, but we've grown and added to the understanding we had in the 1800s.

If I saw you frustratedly trying to bang two rocks together to get a spark and I have a lighter, I'm going to hand you that lighter and say, "You don't have to do that anymore. We have better tools."

The same goes for our relationships. You don't have to stay in unhealthy relationships if you don't want to. There are better tools.

And now that you have access to some better tools, I'm challenging you to use them.

Settled Self

When we understand that leadership isn't grandiose, we begin to see a new landscape on which we can style and build a life that fulfills us at a core level. This sort of leadership costs us our pride; it makes us get off our butts and address parts of ourselves we may have never thought to examine. Embracing an empathetic orientation allows us to establish new relational security—unconditional, reliable security, not the kind that depends on performance, perfect behavior, or topical and flimsy relationships. In the end, aligning our motivation, action, desires, and strategies to be more selfless sets us in a long-desired place of integrity and respect.

When I speak of this *place,* I'm talking about a relational space to live wherein your interactions with those you love leave you fuller and not depleted. I'm speaking of being at a *place* in your life where you walk into the room and feel the respect you've already invested by way of contribution and understanding. This respect is fertile ground on which to build a reputation in your vocation and pursuits. Even more, my hope for you is to be so used to and flexible by way of leaning out and stretching selfless muscles that you do so without even thinking. When this motivation settles in us and our sight line changes from surface level to a deeper understanding, we speak to comprehensive health. We are then not left playing whack-a-mole with individual behaviors, personality traits, and mere differences. We also end up eliminating the blind spots of unawareness that can keep us from the relational world we want. We're instead settled in ourselves.

Calcified or Fortified

When selflessness doesn't come online in us, and we remain in our own vortex of selfish behavior, that selfishness becomes more pronounced as we age. I know I don't need to tell you the permissions we give our elders to be exactly who they are. Because we know the amount of life they've lived, the years under their belts, we excuse and give allowances for behaviors we might not tolerate in other people. Loud talkers who never learned how to modulate their volume for the sake of others become yellers. Those who rarely cared about how their comments made others feel now feel entitled to always share exactly what they think. People who harbor secret bias or prejudice become intolerable as they desperately try to ward off progress.

It's particularly beautiful, then, to see the most selfless and empathetic among us age and to see those qualities become more pronounced, to see them become the truest version of who they've always been. Let's think back to Mrs. Betsy, who was revealed in the end to be of the same purity of heart she always was—just expressed differently than when I knew her as a child. I saw that same character prioritized and lived out into my adulthood, even with sickness and old age physically weakening her. Mrs. Betsy may have been frail in body right before her passing, but she remained as strong as the tallest tree I've seen. Her life was a consistent and clear picture of one living a life leaned out to others. To this day, years after her passing, I still respect the quality of how she lived and how she loved others. Unhealthy relational practices calcify a life and healthy ones fortify and extend it long after we leave Earth. It's up to us to choose what parts of ourselves we want to be magnified. What we cultivate in life is what truly remains of us when we're gone.

My grandmother battled Alzheimer's disease and her last couple of years, albeit painful and devastating to witness, showed me a beautiful reality. As much as she lost her ability to communicate what I knew she had in her head, and although she didn't know my name at the end, she knew that she loved me, and I could feel it in the smile she gave; her eyes could never tell a lie. A while before she passed, I remember hearing about a visit my aunts had with her. At that point, she really wasn't able to communicate clearly and was beginning to lose the larger part of her functionality. But there was a piano in the living room.

My grandmother was a classically trained pianist and a coloratura soprano. Music was such a large part of her life, but as life progressed, she wasn't able to pour as much time and passion into it as she once did. She made her life about her family and loved them, as well as so many others, as best she could. Then, as so many of us do, she let what was once a dream fade to the background of a reality that needed to be met. She laid down her passions and practices to pick up others. Because of this, her musical side was a spark I'd always heard of but regretfully didn't know firsthand.

But one day, while my aunts were there spending time with someone who was now a nearly unrecognizable mother, a beautiful thing happened. My grandmother slowly made her way to the piano and sat down. She began playing from memory a catalog of her favorite songs. She didn't have all the words, but she had the songs in her hands. Her fingers were able to extend and stretch to hit the chords from her past, and, for a moment, my aunts had a window into her practiced passion. It jumped out without the rest of her needing to even be aware of it. It was as much a part of her as her unforgettable laugh. Although her mind couldn't clearly connect to the words she wanted to say, her memory and her practiced skill came to her hands and allowed her to play. Her passion, one she'd laid down, began to pull the rest of her to life in that moment. Trauma may stay in the body, but hear me, so can fine-tuned skill and chosen passion. It's not cheesy or trite or overly simplistic. We get to instill in ourselves, and in those around us, a passion and practice for holistically loving others where they are. This practice can become as second nature as a seamless golf swing, artisan craft, or beautiful guitar riff.

After all, learning a brushstroke or finger placement for a guitar chord is a skill no different than learning how to engage with others well. It's meant to be practiced—not correct all the time, but always in pursuit of better. Relationships are the same: a practice. Relational perfection is not a goal any of us can even have in sight. I hate to tell you, it doesn't exist. Knowing perfection isn't possible takes the pressure off being perfect. The goal isn't perfect people; it's imperfect people marked by a healthy community. A community whose needs you serve as you're able and allow to serve you in return, not out of expectation but out of genuine symbiotic relationship—one that's mutually beneficial.

You can contribute to that health wherever you are, and, without needing others to be perfect first, you can show them deeper and greater health in their own lives. You can lead others to the very healthy and relationally fulfilling place you've longed to see yourself.

We began this book with a conversation about selfishness and looking at comprehensive relational dynamics through a lens of meeting others. Now, we're ending with the lens you see yourself with. Are you a leader, willing to do relational work to set you in the places you want to be down the road? Are you content where you are? Have you possibly become complacent in living in a biodome protected from the wind of others?

There's always another way to meet a person, another way to impact our relational worlds for the better, but we have to look for and grab hold of it. Before I say, "See ya later, friend," I'd like to leave you with a couple of challenges. Instead of a list of opportunities (as we've done in other chapters) to end our time together, I want to simply pour some courage into you. You have more tools now than you did when you started reading this book, and hopefully some new vantage points to consider. Use them.

You've cared enough about your own relational growth and world to finish this journey, but this is just the start. I believe you're meant to be a big tree of a person. I believe you're someone who walks confidently in their life and can do so while looking for ways to meet others with empathy. I believe you're meant to lead where you are and where your heart desires, if you're willing to steward the people you meet along the way. Your career goals, your work, and your relational pursuits are not wholly separate places in your life; they're different parts of the same ecosystem. The health or unhealth in one area affects the atmosphere in all. You have the ability to lead and love those around you. Each time you choose a healthier relational tool than you have before, relational new growth happens, and eventually you see relationships marked by the health and longevity you want in life. You have no idea the joy and settled happiness waiting for you when you decide to live a life designed to meet others—with eyes up and hands out.

I'd like to take you back now to the introduction of this book. Remember that hypothetical café and cozy booth we met at and have been sitting in for the last ten chapters? Well, after all this time together, you now know what I absolutely believe to be paramount: we have to read the room, love the room, and do so with our lives. It's the thing I couldn't leave you without relaying. I can't wait for you to take and build on the reality that people are worth knowing and loving well. *You* are worth knowing and loving well. Consider my writing this book as an attempt to give you a small contribution, a down payment on the life you can establish. I hope you use it to build a lavishly full life for yourself, one marked by deeply fulfilling relationships and character that lifts up and upholds the deepest desires and pursuits of your heart. I mean that, and if I could look you square in the eyes right now, I would.

As we hypothetically stand up now to hug, high-five, fist-bump, or merely smile and acknowledge each other (for those less inclined to physical touch), we begin walking toward that same spiral staircase we came up. Only this time, you're going first and not following me. You know the way. Each step down is like seeing each chapter finished. Yes, that first step you took coming to this conversation was in leaning out to meet me, that was your starting point. Now, as you traverse down that same staircase, you're doing so with a deeper understanding and broader tool belt. You're meant to read the room, and you're meant to build bridges and bend toward others. You can't unknow that now. It's going to change the way you walk out the door, the posture of how you stand in a room, and the way you move through the world outside that door. So I leave you here with an invitation that looks like a door ajar. See the light pouring in through the windows, trying to break through the doorframe to find you? That door cracked open like an invitation—open it and walk out into the world.

Acknowledgments

TO MY INCREDIBLY FAITHFUL, LOVING, and constant parents, Jimmy and Kirie: Thank you for your unwavering patience and for the tenderness with which you love me. Anything fruitful from this book, and from my life altogether, is indelibly tied to your selfless pursuit to love me and others with your whole lives. From the very base of who I am, thank you.

To my siblings, Jonathan, Kayla, and Nathaniel, I love each of you and want to thank you for your investment into my life. Thank you for your faithful love, open arms, and for the incredible nieces and nephews I have the opportunity to love because of y'all.

To my nieces and nephews, Georgia, Sadie, Charlotte, Adelaide, Jackson, Piper, Judah, Evelyn, Eliza, and Bennett, I am forever and always your Cannonball. I'm in your corner and never more than a text, call, drive, or flight away. Your lives are already bright and wondrous. I'm honored to cheer you on in your journeys.

To my people, the ones who have faithfully walked in friendship with me, thank you. Your continued relationship, trust, kindness, support, and unwavering love toward me has meant all the difference in my life. For every late-night phone call, every needed hang, every trip that felt like a deep breath, every joke or bit that sent me into hysterics, for every time you listened to me talk through this book and how I wanted to present it, for every reassurance you gave and every necessary kick in the pants—thank you.

To Nick and Priyanka, thank you for not only standing by me in friendship and life, but for tangibly supporting this message, my heart to deliver it, and my ability to do so. I don't take it lightly or with anything other than gratefulness. Thank you.

To Carolyn, my incredible literary agent and friend, I am beyond thankful for you. Thank you for your patience and steadfast support at each step of this process. You have walked arm in arm with me from the first time we talked about this process. Thank you for every chat, note, edit, hard question, every encouragement given, and for the calm you brought me in the middle of a stressful season. Grateful doesn't cut it.

To my editor, Rachel, and the rest of the incredible BenBella publishing team, I could not have dreamed up a better partnership or team to work alongside for a project of this scope. You have been kind, thorough, trusting, transparent, and wholly a joy to collaborate with. That goes for each incredible member of the team. Thank you for building such a beautiful publishing house to partner with, Glenn Yeffeth. Beyond that, thank you for seeing value in this content and in me sharing it.

About the Author

Cavanaugh James is a speaker, relational equity coach, host of the *Read the Room* podcast, and a perpetual entrepreneur. The common thread of his endeavors is always the same: helping people courageously navigate self-image, healthy relationships, and the ups and downs of chasing a dream.

As a coach to organizational leaders and a sought-after advisor for highly successful achievers, Cavanaugh is dedicated to sharing his insight with anyone who wants something more. Listen to his podcast, *Read the Room*, and connect with him on Instagram to keep the conversation going.